RESPONSE TO ON THE MOVE

I was challenged by the events that took place on the JOC travelled, and later comprehensively described, by Bridget here. Her zealous retelling and reflection have roused me to revisit and further develop what I am willing to believe about healing. Bridget explains her experience with insight, seizing to climb to the unsighted summit (even at the worst of times!). I love this story. I hope you'll enjoy adventuring to Nepal, with Bridget and Greg to disinter the Lord's mysteries.

CARMEN PEREZ, BEnvSc, Master of Teaching

In this beautifully written inspirational book, Bridget shares her 10-day personal journey of faith and prayer with Impact Nations. Witness the power of God through the prayers of ordinary people. Read of the miracles of healing, both physical and spiritual, as they minister to the villagers, hungry to hear about the one and only God.

A must read if you have ever doubted that healing, through The Holy Spirit, is relevant today.

HEATHER LEIGH, Registered Nurse, Certified Midwife

I enjoyed Bridget's honest recount of her trip. She includes warts and all. Her doubts, processing of emotions and triumphs are captured in a very readable style. Her account has made it seem possible for any ordinary person, who wants to serve Jesus in a mission overseas, to achieve this goal.

I liked the way she shared her genuine questions and frustrations, which were ones I could imagine having. Bridget Has a way of making you feel as if you are there with her.

One thought she expressed captured my imagination. Despite moments of perplexity, her conclusion was, 'that we can unequivocally persist in pursuing the mystery of Christ!'

PAM O'HARAE, LLB, Master of Counselling

This true story captures the imagination from the start. It clearly describes the range of emotions felt at the possibility of going on such a journey; the questioning of whether God could still use the author to fulfill His purpose; the excitement of planning and preparing and eventually, of flying to Nepal.

It describes how each day was spent in stillness and prayer – handing over the work ahead to God in His wisdom and power. I loved the clear descriptions of culture, food and customs as well as different places – how the Nepalese were dignified, gracious and hospitable. True connections were made.

Word pictures of miraculous healings and true worship abound along with deep and heartfelt prayer.

The book is written with humor, vulnerability and openness. It shows how we can all be used by God if we yield to His will and allow Him to do His work.

I highly recommend this book as an engaging account that will draw you in from the first pages.

SARI PADDISON, Member of I.J.M. - International Justice Mission, Australia

ON THE MOVE

Journey of Compassion - Nepal

BRIDGET BONNER

On the Move
by Bridget Bonner

Copyright © 2025 by Bridget Bonner

All scripture quotations marked *(NLT)*, unless otherwise indicated, are taken from the Holy Bible, New Living Translation.

Publisher Information
BRIDGET BONNER
The Central Coast
N.S.W.
Australia

For more information or to contact the author, please email
bgeraghty_1@hotmail.com.

ISBN 978-0-6452676-4-8 (softcover)
ISBN 978-0-6452676-3-1 (eBook)

Cover design: Bridget Bonner
Cover photo by Greg Bonner
Interior layout: Justin Shreeves
All testimonies are used with permission

The author's net royalties from this book will go toward promoting the Gospel through, 'Impact Nations.'

First printing: 2025

Printed in Australia

To Greg,
My forever soul mate
and
best friend.

CONTENTS

FOREWORD

Welcome to *On the Move: Journey of Compassion – Nepal*, the beginning of an extraordinary journey—both literal and figurative. This book marks the start of a series that delves into the transformative power of compassion, exploring unique stories from across the globe.

Nepal, a land steeped in kindness and profound spirituality, felt like the perfect place to embark on this adventure. Amid its breathtaking landscapes, I found myself reflecting on invaluable lessons gathered along the way. Each chapter reveals moments of human connection, resilience, and hope amid life's challenges. Through these pages, I invite you to walk alongside me as I witness lives transformed—not only those I served but my own as well.

This book lays the foundation for a collection of stories that will transport readers to new destinations. Together, these narratives will form a tapestry of experiences woven with threads of compassion and understanding. My hope is that they resonate deeply and inspire you to join me on future journeys to discover the beauty of humanity's shared experiences.

Thank you for embarking on this adventure with me.

MAP OF NEPAL

(www.bing.com)

INTRODUCTION

Grateful for the opportunity to complete a Journey of Compassion (JOC) in Nepal, and to be included in the spread of the gospel, I felt compelled to share all about it. I am astonished that miracles still happen in the twenty-first century and that God gave me, (as He does all believers) the privilege, and the authority to share my faith. It's through this sharing, that others will also believe. This book will offer you, the reader, the opportunity to exercise your faith and to be an eyewitness of such miracles.

A detailed and humorous description of how God is enabling ordinary people, like me, to make a difference in developing countries, is given. If you are willing to take on the challenge and to use your freedoms, resources and opportunities to be His hands and feet, God will not only use you, but He will also empower you, to *'GO'* and to share the hope that is within you.

If you have ever had the desire to share your faith, but you've also had reservations, God can remove any obstacles that may be in your way, simply because, He has an even greater desire to include you as His co-worker with Him.

This personal eyewitness account, as well as the testimonies of others, will encourage and inspire you to see, just how much you are blessed. Why? This is the question that must follow … Why are we so abundantly blessed? Surely it is so that we may be a blessing to others!

By the end of this JOC, I discovered that I had received more than I could ever have possibly given!

And he who has seen has testified,
his testimony is true;
and
he knows that he is telling the truth,
so that you also may believe.

(John 19:35 King James Version)

Chapter One

IMPACT NATIONS

*M*y journey of compassion began six weeks before I boarded the plane. I am tempted to say, 'our journey', but no! Even though I went with Greg, my husband, we both had our 'own' separate journeys. I never contemplated going on such a trip until the morning I heard Lesley speaking about an extraordinary experience she had had on a similar trip to the Philippines. It was a typical morning at our 'Know Your Bible' (KYB) meeting, when Lesley took the opportunity to share about her recent experience. With great enthusiasm, Lesley spoke of a young Filipino girl she had prayed for during her trip. This ten-year-old girl was deaf from birth and could neither speak nor hear, she could only make incoherent sounds. Rather than try to reiterate Lesley's testimony of what she saw with her own eyes, she has kindly contributed her own description of what happened.

Testimony: Lesley Hunter

This is my experience in the Philippines of God's Holy Spirit working in the life of a young girl named Hazel.

My husband Michael and I have been fortunate to go on several Journeys of Compassion with Impact Nations since 2017.Our most recent Journey was a 19-day trip in May 2023, to the Philippines, where I witnessed three miracles.

The first miracle happened even before the trip to the Philippines began! It was back in Uganda in September/October 2022, when Steve Stewart, the founder of Impact Nations, asked us all at breakfast one morning, to start asking younger people to come on future Journeys of Compassion. Although we were enjoying serving God in this way, we were all getting a little older.

My first thought was, 'Well how are we going to do that?' I was thinking of our children, all working and our grandchildren, all at school?'

Well, God blew me away by answering our prayers for the next generation to join Impact Nations. Two of our nine grandchildren, Seb (17) and Kiesha (14), and their mother Emma, asked if they could come with us to the Philippines.

Never doubt what God can do even if you think it is impossible.

The second miracle happened during the Philippines trip. There were 44 team members, with 14 families - double the number on previous trips. The 22 children ranged from ten years to nineteen years old. Visiting 20 communities on 7 ministry days, we served 2,500 children with meals and 3,000 people were given access to clean water through the distribution of 180 water filters. In all, 320 miracle healings were recorded.

As is common with most Journeys of Compassion, after our worship time, we were allocated to a specific group for that day – for example – if we were running a medical clinic, nurses and doctors were needed to examine the sick, as well as runners to organise and escort them to the pharmacy. Meanwhile, the remaining team members were allocated to children's games, water filters, and prayer teams. On this Journey we were not running a medical clinic, so only water filters, children's games, feeding children and prayer were run by the Impact Team along with interpreters.

Without doubt, most people want to be on the prayer team to witness the Holy Spirit healing and restoring physically or spiritually.

On this particular day, I was allocated to water filters. 'Well, I won't see any miracles today.' I thought. How wrong I was! God is always full of surprises!

We were in a small village with Christina (Tim Stewart's wife), Maeve and I, plus our wonderful and enthusiastic interpreter. We had just finished assembling and demonstrating how to maintain the water filter, when the man who was in charge of keeping the water filter cleaned and working, asked us if we would go to his home to pray for his daughter. Our little group went next door and discovered that his daughter, Hazel, who would have been around 10 years of age, had not heard or spoken since birth. She sat on a chair outside their humble dwelling, timid and frightened and looking down to the ground with her head drooping to one side.

Long, lengthy prayers were not possible, since hundreds of people each day required prayer. During our two-day orientation, the acronym 'ALICE' was suggested.

This was taught so we could all be on the same page, and to help us remember how to include some important points in our prayers for the sick.

ALICE
A – Ask what they want prayer for
L – Listen for the Holy Spirit
I – Invite the Holy Spirit
C – Command healing in Jesus Name
E – Evaluate the problem and if there is slight healing or no healing, pray again to a maximum of three times.

If healing did not occur after praying three short prayers, then we were to bless the person and move on. Healing may occur much later. Well, we did all that, and after three times of praying over Hazel, asking for the Holy Spirit to heal her, nothing changed. We were so disappointed, and our hearts ached that this little girl may go through life not being able to speak or hear.

I felt that all these people crowding over her must have been scary for her, so I suggested that we all move away and let her father put his hands on her ears. I felt compelled to sing the song 'The Goodness of God' - Christina, Maeve and our interpreter, Emeliana, joined in. We then prayed again from a distance with Hazel's dad's hands on her ears. It was then that Hazel's father said, in a soft voice, 'Hazel.' To our astonishment joy and ecstasy, we saw Hazel look up into her father's face and say, 'Pappa!'

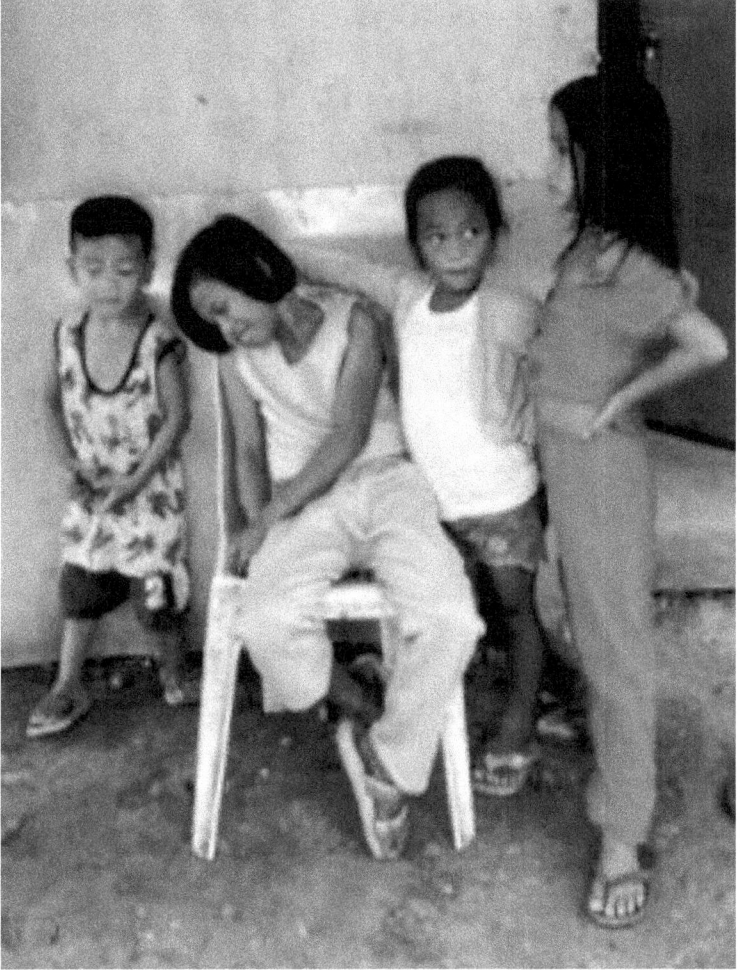

HAZEL BEFORE PRAYER!

PRAYER TEAM WITH HAZEL AFTER PRAYER (LESLEY HUNTER IN WHITE PANTS)

We jumped with joy with excitement, and absolute amazement that the prayer we so urgently prayed was answered. We had hoped to hear her say something else, but she ran off to be with her friends. We were elated and filled with joy, and we and joined the others wanting to share what the Holy Spirit had done.

On returning home, doubts came into my mind, questioning, 'Was that just a one-off situation that Hazel spoke?'

'Can she say any more words, or was that the only word she will ever speak?'

In my morning prayers, I prayed, 'Please Lord, may this not be a one off, but may Hazel continue to speak and hear so her life will be changed for the better.' I'd left it in

God's hands, thinking that I would never know the answers, and doubting the extent of Hazel's healing.

Well, that's when the third miracle happened several weeks after returning home. We received a message on our Philippines' WhatsApp. This is what it said:

> *'Hey friends,*
>
> *I was in a meeting with the pastors this morning and left feeling very encouraged. The Pastors continue to see fruit from the Journey of Compassion. Many Bible study groups have been started and they recently returned to visit the prison, where they were once again allowed to share the gospel and install two water filters. They even delivered the basketball that we left behind.'*

I was so excited to hear the next part of the message, which said,

> *'The pastors were recently in the Barangay village, where that little girl spoke for the first time. Many people ran up to the local team who always wear their blue Impact Nations T-shirts and told them that the little girl is talking so much now!'*

I was filled with anticipation that this could be Hazel, but I wasn't sure, so I wrote back to enquire.

Instantly, Christina confirmed that the little girl was Hazel. Praise God!

I was overjoyed that God heard our prayer for Hazel in the Philippines and that she received complete healing, and God had been so kind to give me the confirmation that I had desired but hadn't asked for. I could feel God's presence covering me with love and kindness, saying, 'Lesley, yes, Hazel is definitely healed.' How kind of Him to confirm my doubts. Oh, the joy and confidence we have in such an awesome God.

Penned by Lesley Hunter 2024

When Lesley passionately expressed her feelings from her Journey of Compassion, I was deeply moved. She had brought me on the journey along with her, I was right there beside Hazel calling in earnest on the Holy Spirit for healing. I was emotionally charged by this eyewitness account of, nothing less than, a miracle. It had been so long since I'd witnessed a miracle, and it left me with a burning desire to find out more.

At the end of our meeting, I asked Lesley a few questions and discovered that the organisation Lesley spoke of was called, 'Impact Nations.' As soon as I arrived home, I initiated my own investigation of 'Impact Nations,' first with a 'Google' search, since Google seems to have all the answers, which led me to the website of the organisation. There was so much information on the 'Impact Nations' website, but straight away, I was drawn in by their mission statement.

IMPACT NATIONS MISSION STATEMENT

Impact Nations partners with leaders in the developing world to rescue lives and transform communities by engaging people in practical expressions of the love of Christ.

Our driving passion is to rescue lives and to see

communities transformed as we demonstrate the love of God. Because God's heart is with the poor, the widow, the orphan and the outcast, Impact Nations goes to the most vulnerable in the developing world. We come in love, with a message of hope, bringing practical expressions of God's compassion and power. We come alongside, working together as a family for lasting change.

(Stewart, www.impactnations.com/our-mission, 2020)

I've always associated true 'Mission', as a calling and commitment to a long-term, if not life-long, assignment and I was immediately impressed that Impact Nations did not actually refer to the trips they conducted as, 'Mission Trips' at all, instead they were called, 'Journeys of Compassion' (JOC). This seemed a much more appropriate name, since some of the trips were as short as only twelve days.

The passion expressed by Impact Nations to rescue lives and see communities transformed, really struck a chord with me. I wanted to be a part of that, but I wondered, 'Am I too old? Can God still use me? Could I make a difference?' I wondered if Greg, would go with me. There were so many reservations I had. My thoughts and feelings ran riot! I needed to talk to Greg, but first I needed to pray and ask for God's guidance. I felt that only God could prepare Greg's heart to be open and willing to go. My heart's desire was that we could go together and experience for ourselves, God on the move, just as we had many years ago in Peru.

Each day passed and each one brought new possibilities of actually doing such a journey. I couldn't stop thinking about it and prayed with new enthusiasm. After much prayer and waiting, I felt more and more positive about the prospect of going on a JOC. Then, something else happened to nudge me along. Sue, another lady from KYB asked, 'Are you interested in the Journeys of Compassion?' Without hesitation, I said in a most definite way, 'Yes, I am.' Sue immediately held up a book and with a radiant smile, she placed the book into my hands and said, 'Read this, I'm going on the next trip!'

That same evening, I began to read the book, 'When Everything Changes,' by Steve Stewart (the Founder and President of Impact Nations). From the very start I was rivetted; it was as though I was right there, an active team member, working in a remote village in the southern part of India. Steve described in pleasant detail, a trip with forty-five very excited people full of anticipation of what Jesus was going to do. I read of the many opportunities to pray for the sick. It seemed that once a healing took place, the villagers came from everywhere with great expectations of further healings. The amazing thing was that this is exactly what happened. The blind received sight, the lame walked and the deaf could hear again. 'Extraordinary!' I thought. Then that old obstinate enemy, 'doubt,' permeated the air I breathed, and the question, 'Really? … Could this really be true?' … resonated like an unrelenting siren.

All throughout the book and in every situation, these healings were attributed to Jesus, and to Him alone. The good news of the Kingdom which the disciples and the early church preached, was once again, being declared right there in India. Its effect was just as powerful at bringing about incredible healing and transformation, as it was in days of old. I really wanted to be a part of this.

Each chapter I read spoke directly to my heart, touching something deep within, stirring memories of the time we had spent on mission in Peru, a time when we lived each day by faith. That time now seemed so distant and dim, yet it was somehow being revived. One by one, I recalled the miracles I had witnessed back then, the joy of God's presence I had felt daily, and His amazing provision. I longed to experience that again. My heart leaped with excitement and expectation. Could I really, in my senior years, experience the power of the radical gospel in action again?

Chapter Two

SOMETHING SIGNIFICANT

I've heard it said, 'Life is the waiting room for Heaven.' How easily I had settled into doing very little, apart from patiently waiting for God's intervention to fix all the problems of the world. I would like to blame the Covid pandemic for my lethargy, after all - the isolation, the prayer and the waiting were reasonable excuses for doing nothing. But what about the past two years beyond Covid? Somehow, over those years my attention had turned, and I lost my focus. My interest in global missions had faded. Covid was the catalyst to blame for that. During Covid I became more and more focused on the overwhelming turmoil in this world. Global poverty, increased child trafficking, ethics around artificial intelligence, anthropogenic climate change, gender dysphoria, overpopulation, scarcity of resources, global economic and political upset, are the major issues that seized my attention and drew me to distraction. I'd been feeling passively unsatisfied by all that Covid had brought with it and I had become very static in waiting for Covid to be resolved.

Then I read Steve's book and his invitation to, 'Participate in something that has significance beyond oneself.' That's when I gained a renewed focus on missions and my new interest sparked enough external force to change my existing state of complacency and move me into action.

In my quiet times, I earnestly prayed for guidance and that God would speak to Greg in the same way as He was speaking to me. In the meantime, I read and read as I waited, hardly able to hide my excitement before talking to Greg about the book. While waiting, I grew more and more confident that God was at work and that this trip could become a reality. I also became more active in my prayer life and began to feel more satisfied in general.

I carefully chose a day that Greg and I had both been fasting. This was something we frequently did together, both for health reasons and for specific prayer reasons. We had always affiliated prayer with fasting as often there was something on our hearts to discuss and pray about. Because we are a blended family, there's always some family matters on both sides to pray for, so that evening we began our dialogue, sharing about family concerns, followed by praying for them. After prayer Greg, being aware of the book I was reading, asked, 'How's the book going?'

Delighted that he asked, I knew this was the right moment and instantly answered his question. 'It's a 'must read,' I said. He could sense the excitement in my voice and wanted to know more. I shared about Lesley giving her testimony at KYB and talked in detail of how her testimony had affected me. I reminded Greg of those very special occasions that we shared in Peru when we were totally dependent on God for everything and how, on occasions we saw unexpected miracles. The memories of how close we had felt to God, every single day, all came vividly flooding back to Greg and me.

With some sadness we reflected on how it all seemed to have faded into the distance. But, like looking at an old photograph, all the memories were rekindled through our discussion elicited by Steve's book. We mused how we seemed to have slipped into a type of lull, a complacency in this land of plenty, where healings through the Holy Spirit's power were rarely witnessed.

I said very little about the content of the book and more about how it left me feeling, that is, 'very excited,' at the possibility of experiencing the things mentioned in it. I then invited Greg to read it for himself and to let me know what he thought. He seemed interested and being an avid reader, was curious enough to accept the invitation.

The next time I saw Sue, I explained that Greg was now reading the book and that we were keen to know more. I also asked in a nonchalant manner, 'When is the next Journey anyhow?'

Sue responded, 'It's in about seven weeks.' My heart sank with disappointment.

'That wouldn't be enough time to organise everything,' I exclaimed.' I was thinking out loud, but Sue ignored me and continued, 'We're going to Nepal.'

'Nepal!' I cried, 'Really!' A sudden surge of excitement ran through my veins. Nepal was and still is, Greg's most favourite place in the whole world. Greg had been on many memorable trips to Nepal with the Rotary Club to do voluntary work. Each time he went, it seemed even better than the last. He loved so many things about Nepal, the culture, the people and of course the landscape. Greg always said. 'It was impossible to go to Nepal and not be in awe of the mountains.' It's true, they are beyond spectacular. So much so, that Greg always managed to mingle a little pleasure after working hard by adding a trek to the end of his trips. Each one of Greg's treks had had a huge impact on his life, which ultimately had drawn him to a saving faith in Jesus. Nepal, with its awe-inspiring mountains and its profound spirituality became a very special place to Greg over the years.

I too, had a soft spot for trekking in the Himalayas. Apart from the Rotary Club trips, Greg and I had been on two of the most amazing treks in the Annapurna Circuit, crossing over the highest pass in the world, 'Thorong La Pass,' (5,416m). Such an incredible blessing to see those mountains close up.

GREG & BRIDGET - THORONG LA PASS, NEPAL

It had been almost ten years since we were last there and I had thought we may never get to go again. This news only added to the interest I already had. I couldn't wait to tell Greg, but first, I wanted to hear how he felt about Steve's book. That evening we sat down to talk, and a lengthy discussion followed. Initially, I asked Greg, 'What did you think of the book?' He had only read up to chapter three. 'I'm not sure,' he said, 'I would love to experience this first hand.'

I responded hastily, 'So would I.' Then followed with a question, 'Guess where the next Journey of Compassion will be?'

'Where?' he said, making eye contact. I hesitated for a moment, 'Where?' he insisted, with a curious tilt of the head, knowing something interesting was afoot. 'Nepal!' I exclaimed excitedly. Immediately his eyes widened, and his smile grew broader. From his expression, I could see this trip to him had suddenly become more personal. 'Hmmm! Really,' he said, with raised eyebrows, immediately followed by the question, 'When?'

'In about five weeks,' I responded.

'Oh! That would be impossible,' he said glumly, 'It's too soon!

'Let's pray about it,' I suggested, 'anything is possible with God.'

After praying we were both totally on the same page. We decided to go for it, with the understanding that, if it didn't eventuate, we would accept it as God's will and not get too upset. Whichever way it went, we were both at peace about it.

I began by registering for the trip and paying the deposit. On further investigation there was much paperwork to complete, but it was all very 'doable.' However, because of the deadline, in the next few weeks, we were swept away in a whirlwind of arrangements. The requirements were many. Firstly, putting together an itinerary, which had to be emailed to Impact Nations before the purchase of flight tickets. Secondly, application of visas for Nepal, followed by purchase of travel insurance, completion of the travel waiver document and background checks, as well as, disclosure authorisation forms, signature of the team unity agreement form, completion of all necessary immunisations and finally emailing copies of all the relevant forms to Impact Nations. We also purchased 'Asia' sim cards to have our mobile phones operating in Nepal. (This was not compulsory; it was our preference). The final and possibly the most vital document was the 'Working with Children Check' (WWCC). We were so grateful that we already had our WWCC completed, as we had been involved in youth and missions' ministries in our church, prior to Covid. If that form hadn't already been completed, the delay would have prevented us from going.

The wheels were in motion for our first Journey of Compassion, and we were very excited at the prospect. The next step was to follow through on the advice to prepare ourselves spiritually. We did this firstly, by watching several teaching videos created by Steve Stewart, which we found to be very helpful.

Next, we needed to complete all the recommended readings, some of which were to help us familiarise ourselves with the norms and customs of Nepal. Other readings were about tips on how to stay pure and prepare ourselves spiritually. These included being careful of what we allowed into our 'eye gate' by keeping a check on the type of T.V. shows and movies that we watched. The same with our 'ear gate.' We were encouraged to think about what we were listening to and to avoid listening to gossip, criticism and negative conversations. Speech was equally important. We were guided to guard our lips and allow God to convict us of any bad language or upsetting words out of our mouths. Rather, to speak blessing towards others. We were reminded not to fill ourselves with garbage as that garbage would need to come out somewhere on the trip.

But what comes out of the mouth proceeds
from the heart, and this defiles a person.
(Matthew 15:18 English Standard Version (ESV)).

The most challenging tip, was, 'Laying down your rights.' I had never really thought about that and when I did, I realised how difficult that could be for me. Some of those rights suggested were, the right to be understood, the right to your own time, to self-pity, to be offended, to self-justification. Even the right to do what you wanted with your possessions. I had put together a bag including gifts for the children and some newborn baby clothes, which I had hoped to give to someone with whom I had made a meaningful connection. It wasn't easy for me to let go of that hope and to realise that I may never even meet with the recipient.

It was only when I read the rationale for giving up my rights, that I began to understand just how important it was. The reason given for laying down our rights was this, 'Not laying down our rights, we are hanging onto the 'self.' Anything 'selfish' could be used by the enemy to cause disruption, hindrance and resentment. We were not expected to be perfect but when it came to advancing the Kingdom of God, we needed to be deliberate in not giving the enemy any grounds to hassle or even to use us.' That was enough for me to comply!

Making room for God's presence and power made perfect sense to both Greg and me. Many more good suggestions were offered during the application process, one of which was, surprisingly, WhatsApp! We joined the JOC WhatsApp group and, as recommended, we introduced ourselves to the rest of the team. This proved very useful in that we were able to get to know the team, ask questions and encourage each other before we even met. Another good piece of advice was, to create a WhatsApp Prayer group of our own by inviting friends and family who would commit to praying during the lead up to the trip and on each day of the trip. Again, this proved to be an invaluable tool as we were able to inform the prayer group of needs or challenges as they unfolded in real time. Often there are many people who would love to go on a Journey of Compassion but can't. This was one way to include them.

Another way of allowing participation of those who can't go, is through sponsorship. The financial aspect of these journeys can be a stumbling block for some. But Impact Nations actively assists with fundraising efforts. They do this by providing an online platform for sponsorship. This is a fundraising page for individual sponsorship by family, friends, or church family. Another way the organisation helps, is by providing a 'Journey Savings Account,' this is purposely designed to help with consistent saving. We found Impact Nations to be a very thorough and professional organisation. They seemed to have all bases covered, safety of the team being a top priority. Road travel was organised using safe vehicles and local drivers known to the leaders. They even had their own personal Chef to do all the cooking to avoid any health issues among the team.

We had a substantial amount of further planning of our own. Apart from the accommodation in Nepal, which was organised by Impact Nations, we needed to organise a stop-over on our outward trip and on the return trip. This was to maximise our travel by including a visit to our son, Patrick, who lives in Singapore. Kyuwon, his wife had recently given birth to twins, Chloe and Caleb. This was their first experience of parenthood, and we were excited to be able to see them and to lend a hand in some small way.

We completed the final arrangements of our trip, by tagging on some down-time, with other members of the team, who were going to Pokhara. And, of course, we rewarded ourselves with a trek, to finish off well. It was a five-day trek to 'Poon Hill', led by Tara, our faithful sherpa-guide. Tara, who is now the proud owner of his own trekking company, insisted on guiding us himself rather than organising one of his Sherpas to do it. Over the twenty-five years that Greg has known Tara, he had become more than a guide, or a business owner, he had become a good friend to both Greg and me.

God's grace to us was our biggest reward by far, because at the eleventh hour, He enabled us to finalise everything!

Chapter Three

ON THE MOVE: SYDNEY - SINGAPORE

6th October 2023

A few minor challenges presented themselves, even before our arrival in Nepal. The first challenge was getting to the airport. My daughter Anna, who normally drops us off at the airport when we travel, had unexpectedly been deployed to Darwin. Her employer sent a task force to gather votes from the remote outback Australian Indigenous people. The votes were for a referendum called, 'The Voice.' This was a proposal to alter the Australian Constitution, that would recognise Indigenous people through a body that would have been able to make representations to the Parliament on matters relating to Aboriginal and Torres Strait Islander peoples. Surprisingly, it turned out that the proposal was rejected nationally and by a majority vote, in every state and territory, thus being unsuccessful. After the referendum I discovered that many of the indigenous people had expressed that they too were against the proposal. Something I had not expected!

A friend, Julie Turner, when called at short notice, saved the day. Julie picked us up in her super, modern electric vehicle and chauffeured us to Gosford train station. When we pulled up at the station, Julie hopped out of the car and promptly proceeded to the boot. Meanwhile, Greg and I were trapped inside, desperately fumbling around to find the well-hidden door handle. Julie opened the boot oblivious to the fact that we were struggling. We were too embarrassed to say anything. Failing the aptitude test, Greg desperately exclaimed, 'How the hell do you get out of here?'

'I don't know,' I said in frustration, but then, to my relief, I found a wheely thing, which when rotated, magically popped open the door!

Delays on the train to Central Station, was the next hurdle which caused us to miss the connecting train to the airport. Despite the buffer we factored into our travel plans, we didn't have a minute to spare. The process of check-in was painstakingly slow but once completed we walked as fast as we could towards our gate number. Hopping from one travelator onto the next at increasing speed, then suddenly, faced with a rope across the next travelator my momentum made it impossible to come to an abrupt halt, I automatically stepped onto the side which happened to be open. It was the wrong side, and it was moving in the opposite direction. Somehow, after a dramatic jig and a balancing act, I manage to hop off again before falling over. Greg continued without hesitation stepping off the travelator; he was now ahead of me as we scurried alongside the travelator. We were now moving at what seemed like, slow motion. Finally, we arrived, heart pounding and breathless, at gate number sixty-one, which happened to be the very last gate. By the skin-of-our-teeth we made it. Once seated, we were able to relax and breathe easy. The flight to Singapore was uneventful. During the next five hours, before landing, we had time to think and contemplate the possibilities for our time with Patrick and Kyuwon and how we would spend some time with their new twin babies.

We had arranged a house swap in Singapore and were able to stay for seven days on the outward trip. With the house came the benefit of borrowing two bicycles, which we had decided to make good use of. Mainly to keep up our fitness levels for the upcoming Nepali trek in high altitude, but also for transport to Patrick's place.

We were fortunate enough to find a house-swap that was only a thirty-minute ride from Patrick's place. Although it was close, we weren't familiar with the district and didn't have a clue how to get there. But we did have Google maps to help navigate so, what could go wrong?

After a restful night's sleep, we mounted the pushbikes early the next morning and set off with great enthusiasm. The weather started out cooler and, with a fraction less humidity, we thought riding the bikes wasn't too bad. It was a pleasant ride through the 'Rail Corridor', where old railway tracks had been replaced by a lush green off-road bicycle/pedestrian pathway. Early in the ride, we realised that the beautiful ambience only continued for a short two kilometres, before ending. By this time, the sun was scorching hot and the humidity overwhelming. The rest of the ride became quite hostile, with cars and trucks on major roads flying past us. Consequently, we arrived very frazzled, hot and sticky.

The unexpected delight of seeing our grandchildren, made it all worth the stress of the ride. What a blessing to spend some time with Caleb and Chloe, both absolutely adorable; each in their own way. They both seemed to be very advanced in their developmental stages. This was no doubt due to Patrick and Kyuwon's significant focus on early education as well as the amount of one-on-one attention given by each of their respective nannies. Also, the numerous amounts of educational toys and early learning resources in the play area would have contributed to their acute advanced cognition.

On the second day, we set off a little later in the day. The hot steamy weather seemed to have already kicked in, even before we began. We were still heavily reliant on Google maps, which somehow let us down badly this time. We were directed a different way, not the rail corridor. Soon into the ride we found ourselves accessing a complicated dual carriageway which, within a couple of kilometres, led onto an overpass and into a five-lane carriageway. Just when I was feeling that it was a pretty risky endeavour, we traversed up yet another hairy section onto a six-lane expressway that with the weather becoming increasingly hotter and more humid, made for a very stressful and challenging trip. By the time we arrived at Patrick's place, two hours later, both Greg and I were stressed and covered in a lather of sweat. Our clothes were absolutely soaked. Fortunately, we were able to use the showers and change rooms at the swimming pool, in Patrick's Condo, before presenting ourselves in a more relaxed and composed state at his front door.

Again, we spent a wonderful day spoiling Caleb and Chloe with our undivided attention.

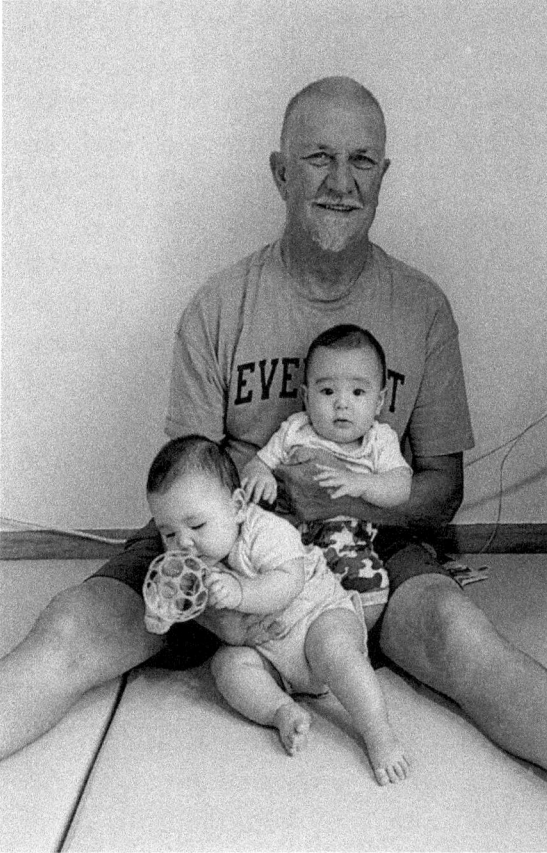

GREG WITH CHLOE & CALEB (SINGAPORE)

We took them for a long walk in the local park, each in their separate strollers. The strollers were surprisingly well equipped with a fan inside the fully enclosed mosquito net attached to the hood. The babies were also doubly protected with insect repellent stickers on their clothes and on the inside of the stroller hoods, as well. Each stroller had padding and support pillows all around the babies, as if they were extremely delicate. It felt like I was pushing a pram with highly sensitive material, which could explode at any moment. The strollers were also heavily armed with a bag attached to the handlebars, packed with nappies, wipes, various creams, a change of clothes, snacks, milk powder, bottles with water and numerous other things including toys.

The walk was quite anticlimactic, we never saw a single mosquito and both babies fell asleep within fifteen minutes of the walk. On arrival back, to everyone's surprize, both Caleb and Chloe were still sleeping and remained asleep in their strollers for a fair spell at the condo.

We set out in plenty of time before dark on the ride home. At least we thought we did! Within the first twenty minutes of riding, in extreme humidity, I felt some relief from some cooling rain drops landing on my skin. Initially, the gentle sun-shower was refreshing. We happily continued riding, but within a short space of time the rain began to pour down. Soon it was so heavy, that the pounding on my helmet became deafening and the giant drops crashing on my arms were almost painful. The sky darkened and the rain ran down the lenses of my sunnies, making it almost impossible to see. Visibility was so bad; it became dangerous to continue. We had to stop and get off before we had an accident. Pushing the bikes in these conditions was absolutely dismal. Just when we though it couldn't get any worse, the place lit up like a roman candle and almost instantly, a terrific clap of thunder followed. We nervously sought cover in a bus shelter and looked at each other bedraggled and sopping wet. Before we could say a word, again, the sky lit up and the glass in the bus shelter shook in its frame with the boom of another thunder bolt. Greg looked at me and said something, but it was as if he was miming. The sound of the rain beating on the roof of the shelter drowned his voice out completely. In disbelief and without saying a word, we both knew then and there, that a taxi in the future might be a better option!

SHELTERING FROM THE RAIN

We used the taxi on each trip to Patrick's place from then on. The week passed very quickly, but very enjoyably, entertaining Caleb and Chloe with the nannies. Because we didn't plan the trip until just a few weeks before leaving Sydney, Patrick and Kyuwon were unable to acquire any time off work. Consequently, they were both working most of the time and we only had a short interlude with them.

We also had some free-time and were able to explore the Railway Corridors at our leisure, during the cooler times of day. We either walked or cycled, without exiting the safety of the corridors, and found them to be a great way of exercising in a lovely natural ambience. On our final evening, as was our custom, we visited Raffles Hotel for a meal and the 'Long Bar,' for a famous 'Singapore Sling,' to celebrate the end of our trip to Singapore. Farewells are never easy, but this time was different since we knew we would be able to visit again on our return trip to Sydney.

Chapter Four

ARRIVING KATHMANDU

13th & 14th October 2023

The five-and-a-half-hour flight to Kathmandu passed quickly as I scribbled down some notes from the reading material we were given. The following is an abbreviated list of tips gleaned from one of the recommended readings.

1. Stay close to God
2. Seek peace (Start speaking blessing now)
3. Do not judge others (Remember the plank in your own eye)
4. Forgive others
5. Guard your heart (and your lips)
6. Obey God's word
7. Be under God's authority
8. Lay down your rights
9. Give away your life
10. Finish well

Eyes closed, I began to ponder, I considered each point over and over, trying to soak-up their meaning. My thoughts rested on point number three, 'Do not judge others.' How hard it is to truly do this. Though I was familiar with Matthew's words on judging others, I wanted to read them again, so I searched on my mobile phone and read them over and over.

> *Do not judge others, and you will not be judged. For you will be treated as you treat others. The standard you use in judging is the standard by which you will be judged. And why worry about a speck in your friend's eye when you have a log in your own? How can you think of saying to your friend, 'Let me help you get rid of that speck in your eye,' when you can't see past the log in your own eye? Hypocrite! First get rid of the log in your own eye; then you will see well enough to deal with the speck in your friend's eye.*
>
> *(Matthew 7:1-5)*

After reading these words repeatedly, I slipped into a world of my own, deep in meditation. Suddenly, a terrifying bump brought me back to earth (literally), the plane momentarily hit the tarmac hard and rough. It became airborne again for a split second before another sudden series of jerks and bumps, then finally…touch down. That had to be the worst landing I had ever experienced. I'm by no means a nervous flyer, but I was glad to get my feet back on terra firma!

In the airport, hordes of travellers, of a diverse mix of cultures moved around in a frenzy of activity. We headed towards the carousels and located our flight number on the second carousel. Surprisingly there was already a mountain of suitcases piled onto the conveyer belt and our one-and-only bag was among them. Travelling light, in anticipation of a short trek at the end of our trip, we only had one carry-on backpack each. However, we also brought one checked-in bag (full of gifts) with the intention of leaving it behind. We grabbed the bag with haste and headed for the exit. What a relief to be soon outside the chaos of the airport where the crowd seemed to disperse a little.

It was hot and noisy but less frantic outside. We moved in the same direction as the rest of the passengers, not really knowing where to go. We just followed the colour-fully dressed group of people who seemed to know where they were going. We were led towards a narrow pathway with railings on either side and people waiting on each side of the railings. Pleasantly surprised, we saw a Nepalese man holding a sign with, 'Impact Nations,' written on it. As we approached him, we were warmly greeted by name and ushered to a nearby taxi. Our driver, speaking English with a distinct Indian accent, was friendly and helpful. He even offered to carry Greg's bag. He was quite talkative and asked about our flight. Once in the car, he was mostly silent during the drive. He seemed to be very focused on the traf-fic. It was dangerously hectic all the way to the hotel. There were so many motorbikes darting in-and-out of cars, some with three people squashed on them, and some with a family of four including two children.

FAMILY ON BIKE

Only the rider seemed to wear a helmet, not the passengers. We also saw two men with a goat on one small motorcycle. There were a few close shaves during the short twenty-five-minute drive. One, where our vehicle brushed a cyclist who barely scraped through the narrow space between our car and the one closely beside us. It was a relief to be dropped off at the 'Northfield Hotel' in one piece.

Arriving a couple of nights early meant that we had time to relax and settle-in before the rest of the team arrived. Our room was basic it was very basic! Having had some past visits to Nepal this was no surprise. A five-star hotel in Nepal is the equivalent standard to a three-star hotel in Sydney, and a three-star is equivalent to a hostel. We were at the three-star level.

STREET VIEW FROM OUR ROOM (KATHMANDU)

After unpacking our few belongings, we decided to have a siesta before setting out to dinner. By the time we set off it was dark, so we decided not to go too far away. We found a typical Nepalese restaurant, the 'Thakali

Kitchen', just a stone's throw from the hotel. This proved to be a good choice as we found one of our favourite dishes on the menu, a 'Thakali Thali Set'. The word 'thali,' only refers to the 'plate' or 'tray,' it's the round silver or bronze tray with small matching bowls (at least six) set around the outside of the tray. Each bowl is filled with a variety of Thakali cuisine, including different curries, vegetables, sour chutney or pickle, curd, spices and a heap of rice placed in the centre of the tray. The best part is a piece of Nepali Gurung bread, a deep-fried flat bread, placed on top of the rice. It's an amazing diversity of tastes and aromas, while at the same time it provides a very nutritious, wholesome meal. To add a typical Nepali feel to the ambience during our meal, mid-conversation, the lights went out. We sat in pitch-black darkness for a few seconds, then we remembered about the blackouts. Nothing had changed in the past ten years!

THAKALI KITCHEN

In spite of the blackouts, three in all, the service was amazing. Even in the dark, a bright flickering candle, carried by a super friendly staff member, made its way to our table. On all three occasions, the candle on our table was lit from theirs, and humble apologies were given, even though it was no fault of their own. Then when the lights came on, the candle was snuffed out, as if not to waste it. I thoroughly enjoyed the whole experience.

We explored the area as we walked back to the Hotel Northfield, discovering a multitude of shops, ATM's, cafes and restaurants, which were all within a short walking distance from the hotel. On arrival back at the hotel, the staff welcomed us with such enthusiasm. All that, plus a full stomach, made the world seem a better place! Even the hotel was looking good as we reflected on the fact that we didn't have to share a room with anyone, and we had our own private bathroom.

However, we soon realised that the hotel was in the middle of a very lively night-life hub in Thamel. The extremely loud traffic noise, the hustle and bustle of tourists, the street sellers and motorbike-revs echoed late into the night. It was sheer madness! The stifling heat of the day continued all through the night, which made it impossible to shut out the noise by closing the windows. We had a choice to die of heat exhaustion or to contend with the noise. We chose the noise, thinking it might stop at some point, but no. It continued into the early hours of the morning, resulting in a sleep-deprived night!

Fairly early the next morning, Greg was feeling unwell, he had a typical case of, 'Delhi-belly' and the poor man was chundering his guts up since dawn. He thought it might have been due to the Thakali food, but I wasn't convinced as I had no symptoms at all. In spite of this rough night, we still headed for the hotel dining room for breakfast. We were surprised to find so many other team members already there.

Although the JOC hadn't yet officially started, many had arrived in the early hours but, like us, they couldn't sleep with the racket outside. Fortunately, we all had another full day to recover from either, Delhi-belly or from sleepless nights, before commencement of orientation. Our team leader, Bill, who oversaw logistics and was responsible for making sure that the trip ran smoothly, was one of the earliest to arrive.

Bill was a confident man, of average height, with a lean, but strong physique. He was a great communicator who, regardless of his size, had an amazing capacity to bear the brunt of everyone's complaints. Behind the trendy black beard and moustache, was a very patient man who was kind in his speech and managed to put up with all of us. He also was able to keep calm in an emergency. Bill was the first one to introduce himself and warmly welcome us into the fold. He asked if we were okay with our room, and by then we had settled in and were satisfied with it. Apparently, there were already some complaints about the hard beds, one or two people even wanted to change their room. Bill very graciously accommodated them.

One person, (Hector) missed his flight to Doha; he managed to rebook a flight, but three hours later his flight was cancelled, and he still hadn't arrived. To buoy him up, the rest of us sent out encouraging messages via the WhatsApp page. Many team members had been travelling for twenty-four hours and more; some from Canada, some from the United States and of course the rest of our group from Australia. Despite the lack of sleep, had by all, I could sense a buzz of excitement in the air. We shared our stories in comfortable conversation which flowed freely to-and-fro, keeping us all awake and animated. We each did our own thing after breakfast, but not without getting the rundown on safety issues, especially while outside the hotel. Greg and I went shopping and later met up with some of the team for lunch. It was a pretty ordinary lunch, and Greg was still feeling off-colour, so we left early, and Greg spent the rest of the afternoon trying to rest and recuperate. I too, welcomed a siesta after lunch, but unfortunately it was short lived due to the incredible heat and humidity.

More team members had arrived by that evening, whom we bumped into randomly and later had the opportunity to chat with in the dining room. Greg and I had an interesting time happily spent mingling among the group, just chatting and finding out more about each other. I came across a number of extraverts able and willing to tell all, as well as some reserved yet agreeable characters, who held their cards close to their chest; each one with his/her own fascinating and diverse personality.

Even though we did little more than chinwag, Greg and I were exhausted by the end of a full day of interaction with our team. Another hot and sleepless night followed in the central location of Thamel, Kathmandu. The atmosphere outside continued to be loud and lively, buzzing frenetically with the sound of a multitude of street noises.

I wondered how on earth I would ever be able to stay awake during orientation the following day.

Chapter Five

ORIENTATION AND TRAINING

*A*lthough we had another night of interrupted sleep, we did at least feel grateful that we'd had a couple of days to settle in, unlike Hector and Joan who only arrived the night before after many hours of being in transit. Just before orientation, we were gathered together in the dining room for breakfast. I scanned the room and spotted Hector immediately; he was the fit looking quintessential Jamaican/American man with a ponytail made up of plaits which dangled over a short-back-and-sides haircut. His hair was black but with a couple of blond plaits mingled in. Hector was standing by himself looking a little dazed, so I approached him and introduced myself. We had a short, easy chat about the fun and games of travelling. Considering the sleep deprivation he'd gone through, Hector looked surprisingly fresh. His neatly trimmed black moustache and beard framed a beaming white smile; he smiled a lot. In fact, I'm sure he never went 40 seconds without smiling. Hector was a very likeable young man in his prime, with a warm and friendly personality. I sensed that he was going to be a great asset to the team.

After some interesting conversations enjoyed over a wholesome breakfast, served at 6.30am sharp, we began our first day of orientation. This commenced with a time of loud and lively worship. With just one guitar and no microphones, our many voices could be heard from all over the hotel, and probably even from halfway down the street. Songs of thanksgiving burst out spontaneously one after another in a beautiful flowing harmony, which seemed to ignite a passion in all of us. There was no need to follow songs on paper, we had them written on our hearts and we were able to collaboratively express our love for God with open sincerity. Each one of us sang with gusto, and the words in turn spurred us on to remember God's faithfulness. It was clear that nothing was held back, our spirits soared in His tangible presence, and we were captivated. This mysterious feeling of being bound together in the rapture of true worship was overpowering. God's presence was powerful and unquestionably real. Words are barely sufficient to describe this close encounter with God. Nothing I could say would hit the mark; you have to experience it for yourself. It was just so wholesome to be with like-minded strangers, united by some supernatural, divine force beyond our understanding. People from many different backgrounds and different parts of the world, yet, all at one with each other through this amazing experience of worship. I was so encouraged.

Enter his gates with thanksgiving and his courts with praise; give thanks to him and praise his name. For the LORD *is good and his love endures forever; his faithfulness continues through all generations.*

(Psalm 100:4-5)

From the very beginning I felt a connection with many of the team members, I had never met before, and we all seemed to bond cross-culturally, very quickly. From Australia there were nine of us, from three different churches on the Central Coast, New South Wales. Beck was younger than the rest of us retirees, but she fit in really well. Everyone loved Beck! There were six Americans across the states of Oregon, New Mexico and Arizona, as well as nine Canadians from Calvary Barrie in Toronto and a couple, Iana and Marcel, from Springwater, Ontario. A total of twenty-four in all. Among the Nepalese partners on the ground, were pastors, several translators, drivers and the lead pastor, Randeep Mathews. Randeep was from India, he was accompanied by his two sons, Arsh and Samuel, as well as his daughter, Prathna, and her husband Isaiah.

Orientation continued with some general instructions from Bill. In his usual confident manner, he informed us that although each day was already planned, the villages that we would be visiting had not yet been made known to him. The partners who worked closely with Bill were invaluable as they knew the village people well, they spoke the local dialect, and they knew the culture and could prepare the villagers for our visit. Bill gave a rundown of the plan for each day of our journey. He provided a more detailed description, what follows is a brief explanation of each day, in a nut shell!

We would spend a second day of orientation in Kathmandu. On day three, we would be facilitating a picnic for a community of young women and their children on the outskirts of Kathmandu and returning to the Hotel for our last night in Thamel. Day four, entailed travelling through Kathmandu and stopping on the outskirts, to visit a Centre, which was home to the young women, from the picnic the day before. Following that visit, we would travel another five hours by coach or jeep, over some rough and dangerous roads, in extremely hot and humid conditions, to Chitwan. There, in a remote village, on the outskirts of Chitwan, we would provide our first medical clinic and distribute water filters. On day five, in a different village, our second medical clinic would take place as well as the provision of water filter. Day six would be a rest day, where a visit to a wildlife park was planned. On day seven, the third medical clinic, in an even more remote village, would take place. On Saturday, day eight, we would be attending a church in one of the villages, with an opportunity to share our testimonies during the service. Day nine would be spent mainly travelling back to Kathmandu, to debrief and pack, ready to finish our Journey of Compassion.

Bill encouraged us to take some travel sickness medication on the long-haul trips and asked us, in the kindest way, not to vomit on the bus, but rather tell the driver to stop the bus.

In his more definite voice, Bill explained that every member of the team would be expected to participate in some important role on the clinic days, whether they had medical experience or not. These roles included crowd control, being a runner, helping in the pharmacy, being part of a prayer team, serving food, and the distribution and installation of water filters in various homes. The mobile medical clinic team comprised of a pharmacist, a midwife (myself), as well as many qualified doctors and nurses; we were all expected to help with the sorting of medications and the setting up of the clinic. Our role included examining and treating or referring patients as well as providing and administering antibiotics, pain relief and other medications.

The whole team were instructed on how to complete a white Registration Card for each individual who presented at the clinic. Each role was described, and we had the opportunity to ask any questions. The job of, 'Runner,' involved escorting patients from one area of the clinic to another to avoid congestion and delays. Both doctors and nurses were to examine the patients and, if needed, refer them either to the pharmacy with a script or to the prayer team for prayer (as requested by the patient). Nurses would be supported with a backup doctor to refer any cases beyond their scope and to confirm that the correct meds had been suggested. The pharmacist would then dispense the meds and refer the patient back to the nurses if a dose needed to be administered immediately.

The medical team were told that they would be given a more detailed description of what to expect on the first real day in action. At the end of our first orientation day, we had a lengthy question and answer time and we were all encouraged to get involved as much as we were able.

It all seemed extremely well organised. To facilitate getting to know one another on a deeper, more collaborative level, we were put into smaller 'Care Groups' of five people and a leader was assigned to each group. We then separated into our respective care group, and were given time to introduce ourselves, share a little and chat about how we were feeling. We did some interesting team building exercises, and were told that we would be meeting up, in our care group, at the end of each day to debrief and to share about our experiences, our highlights or our disappointments. The groups were designed to provide a safe and confidential space, comfortable enough to share anything that we may not be able to share in a larger group. It was quite a morning, information overload for many of us, but finally it was time for a well needed lunch break.

After lunch, we assembled for a session of teaching on prayer, it seemed important that we were all of one mind in regard to prayer. Due to the quantity of Nepalese people expected to present for prayer, it was important to get to the point without wasting time. The way to do this was to provide us all with the same body of knowledge so that we could act in a similar manner when praying for others.

We were given some biblical principles of praying for healing to help us apply precise and relevant prayers in a short space of time. As Lesley mentioned in her testimony (chapter one), the acronym 'ALICE,' was a simple but powerful model of prayer which we were encouraged to use. Lesley gave the meaning of each letter in point form, but I will endeavour to explain it in more detail.

ACRONYM 'ALICE' EXPLAINED

We were instructed that the first thing to do, when approached by a person seeking prayer, was to…ASK that person what they specifically needed prayer for. This seemed a little odd to me at first, especially when the problem might be staring me in the face on most occasions. But in reality, I was surprised. For example, one time a woman with a severe limp, hobbled towards me using a stick, but on enquiry as to what she needed, she responded by asking me to pray for her husband! I was taken aback and lost for words, for a moment, I quickly learned not to assume anything from then on, but to clarify the request in order to get a clearer understanding of what the person really wanted.

Next, was to…LISTEN carefully. We were instructed that to listen effectively, we needed to be active and intentional in our listening. A brief run down on how to do this was given, with an opportunity to ask questions. First and foremost, we were to listen to the person with undivided attention. Due to the use of translators, I found this to be very tricky. When I listened to the person asking for prayer in their own language, apart from the tone of his/her voice, it meant very little to me. Most of the time I found that my attention was divided between listening to the interpreter and looking to the person wanting prayer. Once the prayer request was interpreted, it was suggested that an appropriate pause be allowed to get a clearer understanding of the prayer request and to purposefully allow time to listen to God speak.

After a pause, we were to INVITE the Holy Spirit into the situation and ask that God's love would rest on that person, stating his or her name if possible. Another silent pause might follow before asking for God's healing power upon the person.

At the appropriate time, we were urged to invoke the name of Jesus and COMMAND the pain to go, speaking directly into the area of injury, sickness or disease by name (i.e. the part of the body…leg, arm or back) and tell it to be healed in Jesus's name.

The final step was to EVALUATE the injury or sickness by testing it. The main way to do this was by observing for any change in the level of pain or mobility or by visual appearance of the wound/sickness. And by asking the person whether he/she felt any change or could confirm any improvement.

The principles of prayer were only a guide to the 'novice prayer' and mainly given to help us all keep focused on the Holy Spirit. I felt that the acronym ALICE provided a simple yet ingenious method of concise prayer.

It was so good to hear that we were the ones expected to pray for the sick, that if given the opportunity, we were the ones expected to lead people to Christ. It was said too, that the work of the Holy Spirit is not limited and if we felt led by the Spirit, and stirred with compassion to lead people to Christ, then we should confidently do so. We were reassured on the other hand, that there was always a local Nepalese pastor available if we needed support in the area of faith.

Orientation continued with the distribution of team T-shirts and I.D. badges, followed by the sorting and labelling of medications and the organising of the gifts brought by each individual team member. This turned out to be a mammoth task as there were numerous medications and many suitcases full of gifts.

The gifts comprised of various toiletries including eco-friendly sanitary products, toys, skipping ropes, balloons, bubbles, hand puppets, all manner of stationery, baby clothes, good quality second hand clothes and a multitude of other items.

Our time of orientation was rapidly coming to a close with a more detailed rundown of the activities for the following day's program. Bill handed over to Pastor Randeep, a confident middle-aged man who spoke with a strong Indian accent to explain the plan of action. His thick dark eyebrows and short black hair, greying at the temples, gave him the (older) George Clooney look. He appeared to be at home in his dark olive skin, comfortably aging well.

Pastor Randeep explained that the plan was a picnic in the park for a group of young women and their children. Games were to be organised to entertain the children while their mothers had a break and were, hopefully, being engaged in conversation with members of the team. He asked us to consider what we hoped to contribute and to pray about how we could interact with the women and the children. Although we were all encouraged to participate in some way or another, no one was allocated to a specific task, it was a wait and see how it all pans out situation.

A number of the team were to serve the food provided by Impact Nations, which was cooked by a Nepali chef, who was part of the Impact Nations team. Everyone, including all the team members, were to be fed, at least one-hundred people or more.

While no demands were made of us, we were all encouraged to step out of our comfort zone. Pastor Randeep explained that he would preach the word and lead in a time of worship, his hopes were that we would participate in the worship and where appropriate, pray for anyone who asked for prayer. He added that it was okay to share our own story if we felt led to do so.

In fact, his core emphasis all through orientation, was that we would just listen and love people. Pastor Randeep concluded our first day of orientation by announcing that there would be an optional teaching and prayer session commencing at 4am, the very next morning. Yes 4am! We were then let loose to enjoy some free time for the remainder of the evening.

Our small group, Sue & Murray, Anne & Arthur, Lesley & Barry and ourselves, all from the Central Coast, decided to share a meal together, to celebrate the fact that we all managed to stay awake and engaged in the day's briefings. However, being in our sixties and seventies, we unanimously agreed that all of us desperately needed a nanny-nap beforehand!

Thamel is a pre-Base Camp venue for mountaineers, and no matter the time was always swarming with tourists and locals alike; that evening was no different. The restaurant we had booked was not far away, nonetheless, walking in a group proved to be quite a challenge. The narrow pavements were limited and often non-existent in places, leaving the hordes of people with no alternative but to spill out onto the busy roads and walk alongside frantically moving traffic. To make things worse, there were bicycles and rickshaws everywhere with motorbikes and cars darting their way in and out of sticky situations. Even the odd horse-drawn carriage managed to, somehow, weave its way through the narrow winding roads. After a few close escapes from nearly being run over, we decided it was an impossible death trap. Thankfully, although a little unravelled, we did make it to the restaurant still intact.

STREET IN THAMEL WITH LESLEY & BARRY

On stepping into the peaceful restaurant, I'm sure we all felt an instant escape from the bustling chaos of Thamel, I know I did. I breathed a sigh of relief, content to be out of the noise and confusion of traffic. Our group quickly settled down in the quiet haven of the restaurant. The Nepali menu was starkly different to anything we could find in Australia.

I loved the variety and the spices used in Nepal, but not everyone in the group did. Murray in particular, in his own words said that he had, 'the taste buds of a toddler.' He liked very bland food and didn't tolerate the spices well at all. In other ways Murray was an adventurous man, especially on the water in a kayak. Kayaking was his forte but here in Nepal his delicate tolerance to spicey food was his Achilles Heel. He mainly ate rice throughout the duration of the trip.

We ordered our meals and had some lively conversations reflecting the day's events. The evening quickly sailed by and although we were all excited and animated about the next stage of our trip, we decided to call it a night.

Our contribution to provide aid on the 'Journey of Compassion,' was about to begin and we couldn't wait.

Chapter Six

PICNIC IN THE PARK

16th October 2023

Although breakfast wasn't served until 6.30am, my day began somewhat earlier with the gentle sound of my phone's alarm. Greg muttered, 'What time is it?'

'3.40am' I whispered as he groaned and rolled over showing no further signs of life, apart from a quiet snore. Greg was still not fully recovered and although Delhi-belly doesn't sound like much, it does take the wind out or your sails. I was wide awake and jumped out of bed immediately. After dressing and splashing my face as quietly as I could, in the dark. I was ready for a time of biblical teaching and prayer. Although this was an option, not requisite, I was determined to attend every day, no matter how sleepy I felt.

The room allocated for prayer was on the next level. I walked up one flight of dimly lit stairs, which grew darker as I got to the top. It was so dark that I couldn't find the light switch. I activated my phone torch. I searched the walls and was able to locate the switch. Nobody was there. My first thought was, maybe I was on the wrong floor, or perhaps I had misunderstood the start time. I waited just a minute or two, then Pastor Randeep arrived. I was glad to see him, though he looked a little rough, like he hadn't slept all night. After greeting one another, we waited quietly for a few moments hoping someone else would arrive. Two others soon arrived and they too looked a little stunned and sleepy. At this point, (realising that it was too dark to look in the mirror) I wondered how I looked... perhaps the same or possibly even worse!

As we waited for more people to arrive, Pastor Randeep was very respectful of each one of us, not elevating himself, he asked us to call him by name rather than 'Pastor'. His friendly personality made you feel comfortable and at ease as we engaged in friendly conversation. When one other person arrived, apologising for her lateness, Randeep warmly welcomed her in a softly spoken voice, assuring her that she hadn't missed anything. He then began by asking each of us to read a small section of the scriptures. We read aloud from the book of Ephesians.

So, I tell you this, and insist on it in the Lord, that you must no longer live as the Gentiles do, in the futility of their thinking. They are darkened in their understanding and separated from the life of God because of the ignorance that is in them due to the hardening of their hearts. Having lost all sensitivity, they have given themselves over to sensuality so as to indulge in every kind of impurity, and they are full of greed.

That, however, is not the way of life you learned when you heard about Christ and were taught in him in accordance with the truth that is in Jesus. You were taught, with regard to your former way of life, to put off your old self, which is being corrupted by its deceitful desires; to be made new in the attitude of your minds; and to put on the new self, created to be like God in true right-eousness and holiness.

(Ephesians 4:17- 25)

Randeep then shared what he said was one of his favourite stories. It was a fable taken from a Native American folktale, 'The Eagle or The Chicken.' Shortly into the telling of the story, the door opened, and another member of the team hastily entered the room. A young lady, appearing quite anxious and looking a little bedraggled, apologised profusely. Again, Randeep warmly welcomed her with gracious words and calmly ushered her to take a seat. He then began by starting at the beginning of the story in a relaxed manner and he seemed totally undisturbed.

The gist of the fable was about identifying and conquering the things that hold you back from becoming a better version of yourself. The narrative was of an earthquake which caused an eagle egg to roll down a mountain out of its nest and into a chicken farm. The egg was placed with the chicken eggs by the farmer and consequently hatched and grew up with the chickens. The tale compared the life of a nearsighted chicken scratching in the dirt for food, with the life of an astoundingly sharp-sighted eagle, soaring high above the ground with a good choice of food to choose from. The ultimate question being, 'Do you want to be the chicken or the eagle?' In other words, are you satisfied in settling for a comfortable and mediocre church life serving your own community, or are you willing to risk spreading your wings to be carried by the Spirit of God to help your fellow man across oceans?

We had, apparently only made the first step, but now it was time to discover ways in which we could apply the truth that comes from knowing Jesus. This involved acknowledging that our old life was sinful by nature, that since we had accepted Jesus as our Lord and Saviour, we had been given the Holy Spirit. Because of this gift of the Holy Spirit we now have the power to cast off this sinful nature. Randeep talked about how to avoid giving the devil a foothold. We read Ephesians a second time with a focus on the following verses,

> 'So, stop telling lies. Let us tell our neighbours the truth, for we are all parts of the same body. And "don't sin by letting anger control you." Don't let the sun go down while you are still angry, for anger gives a foothold to the devil.'
>
> *(Ephesians 4:25-27)*

We talked in depth and prayed together, asking the Holy Spirit to help us to grow this new nature of being more Christ-like, by renewing our thoughts and attitudes. We were encouraged, when we pray, not to be afraid of failure, but just to be faithful in prayer and fully trust in Jesus to work through us.

I came away richer for having had the study and the conversations; the prayer too, was uplifting and quite liberating. I felt fearless and unafraid because of a greater awareness of the Holy Spirit at work in me, rather than me trying to do the work.

I was so energised that when Elizabeth asked, 'Does anyone want to go on a prayer walk?' I immediately accepted. We arranged to meet around 5.30am in the foyer of the hotel. The short time in between, I spent in my room catching up with Greg and sharing some of the teaching. But it slipped away very quickly.

After meeting Elizabeth in the foyer, we began a brisk walk through the slightly quieter streets of Thamel. We walked and talked at the same time. Elizabeth an extremely fit and much younger woman, set the pace, it was no easy task to keep up with her. Our conversation flowed freely, interrupted with occasional spontaneous outbursts of prayer according to the subject of our conversation. We were both so animated as we powered along, passing interesting wooden and brick structures with intricately carved wooden windows and doors.

Occasionally, I was tempted to stop and take photos, but it would have distracted from the purpose of our walk, and it would have been impossible to catch up with Elizabeth if I did stop. The lighter traffic of the early hours allowed us to move along with great speed; hoping on and off the narrow pavement was the only thing that interrupted Elizabeths momentum. As there was nowhere to step, except into the road I was grateful for the odd motorcycle which slowed her down. The distance between us was getting longer and longer as she raced ahead.

I was out of breath and thankful when Elizabeth finally stopped in Durba Square. Something had caught her eye; Elizabeth had stopped to take a photo of a17th Century Krishna Temple. It was such an interesting place, full of ancient shrines and temples, all with an historical and cultural significance. I quickly began to take some photos and used this opportunity to look at the ancient architecture of the many temples and palaces scattered around the square.

We stumbled across a red-brick three storey building with its fascinating pagoda style roof and palace called, Kumari Chowk. This was the temple used as the residence of the *Kumari*, a virgin girl who is worshipped as a living goddess.

The Kumari is chosen to be a living embodiment of the Hindu Goddess Durga. The child is carried into the temple from the tender age of only one-year-old, (thereabouts) and she is carried everywhere as it is believed that if her feet touch the ground, she becomes impure. The infant remains there, until the age of puberty, when her first menstruation occurs. After which, it is believed that the divine energy leaves her body, and she can no longer be a goddess.

The Kumari is then replaced by a newly chosen goddess. The old Kimari needs to be carried out of the palace as she had never learned to walk. Also, the Kumari is trained never to smile, as it is believed that if she does smile it is a bad omen on the person she smiles at. I was struck by how starkly different the Nepalese customs and beliefs are from ours.

KUMARI CHOWK - THE LIVING GODDESS

I could see a leaning building which was supported by some makeshift scaffolding made out of timber beams. A plaque in front of it said that it was one of the oldest temples to survive the most recent earthquake of 2015. It didn't look safe at all. Apparently, construction of Durbar Square actually began in the 3rd century but due to severe earthquakes, the original buildings were reduced to rubble and the oldest surviving temples only dated back to the 16th century.

16TH CENTURY BUILDING SUPPORTED BY TIMBER BEAMS

The busy square was a haven of local activity, people circumambulating their many idols which were dotted around. Some grasping onto their prayer beads or turning their handheld prayer wheels, others just sitting around and chatting or staring into space. There were street vendors selling their wares, women dressed in colourful saris and several men in long, loose-fitting shirts and pants. I loved the ambience of this place, there was something overwhelmingly spiritual about it.

When I was about to leave the open square, I glimpsed a platoon of uniformed soldiers running towards us. I instinctively grabbed my phone and captured a video as they passed. The soldiers were impressive and intimidating at the same time. Elizabeth had sprinted ahead, and I could barely see her in the distance. It took me a while to catch up as I became breathless on the uphill. I had to stop for a spell, breathing heavily. When I looked around at the unfamiliar surroundings, I felt completely lost. I began to wonder if Elizabeth knew where she was going! I ran hard and fast to catch up with her, calling out for her to stop. Struggling for breath, I was relieved to see that she had stopped. It took a moment to gain my composure before I could speak, then I asked the question, 'Do you know where we are?'

'I've got no idea!' she said panting as she looked at her watch, 'But we can't be too far,' she continued. OK, I mused as I reached for my phone, exclaiming 'We've been walking for nearly an hour now.'

'No stress,' Elizabeth responded, 'We just have to pick up the pace!'

'It might help if we knew where we're going,' I said as I searched in Google maps. I hadn't realised that Elizabeth was just feeling her way around without navigating or tracing where she had been going using an offline map. 'It's still a further ten minutes away and we are already a couple of minutes late for breakfast,' I continued. This time, using Google maps we found our way back, but inevitably we were late. We missed out on the best food, but some of the pickings were still available. Word spread that the coach had arrived. I wolfed down the remains of my modest breakfast and caught up with Greg in our room with barely enough time to go to the bathroom.

All the rushing, as it turned out, was unnecessary. The inevitable situation with a large group of people, was... hurry, hurry, hurry...then, sit and wait. As we sat on the bus waiting for stragglers, it seemed a while since I had sat still, and I suddenly felt very weary.

After a few minutes of white noise and staring into space, I could hardly keep my eyes open. It felt as though I had already done a day's work and it was only 8am. Greg was bright and chirpy but I just wanted to close my eyes and rest. Greg could see that I was tired, so he thoughtfully began chatting with Barry who was sitting in the aisle seat opposite him. I then zoned out and had a chance to close my eyes!

Eventually the bus began to fill up in dribs and drabs as the team made their way to their seats. The temperature was on the increase and the atmosphere rapidly became hot and humid. In anticipation of the poor roads and the forty-five minute ride, it was suggested that we take some ginger tablets. Greg and I rarely experienced motion sickness, but we took them anyhow, just in case.

I couldn't sleep on the bus; I was more excited than I was tired. We were headed to a park in Lalitpur, and my mind drifted to the picnic that we were about to provide. The plan was that the cook, a Nepalese man who worked with Impact Nations, would set up a huge banquet to feed all the women and children as well as the translators, seven in all and the whole team of twenty-six of us. As soon as the bus got started, the aircon cooling the atmosphere made it a pleasant ride which was soon over with nobody getting sick. I put our collective reprieve form travel sickness down to the air conditioning rather than the ginger tablets.

On arrival to the small lush green park, the scene was phrenetic with activity. A huge colourful Marquee provided a shaded area for some chairs where a group of young girls sat in a circle, singing and clapping in unison. There were many women and children of all ages. The older women wore vibrant Sari's, while the younger women dressed in modern jeans and T-shirts. Many children of varying ages from toddlers to early teens ran around chasing each other while older teens, some carrying small babies, were just milling around in the sunshine.

As we headed towards the crowd, the team dispersed, as if being dragged this way and that by unseen hands. Lollipops and other candies began to pass from one to another, and balloons appeared among the joyful smiling faces, but then I caught sight of a small child with a sad face.

I walked towards him smiling, but when he saw me coming, his forlorn and broken eyes pulled away from my gaze instantly. I stooped down and motioned toward the hand puppet dancing on my hand and said, 'Namaste!' The furry animated Kookaburra caught the boy's attention, he seemed uncertain, his face expressing a mixture of fear and excitement as he stared wide-eyed at the bopping Kookaburra. Namaste is the only word I know in Nepali, so I had to revert to English after my greeting was delivered. I thought of the famous Australian Kookaburra rhyme, 'Kookaburra Sits on the Old Gum Tree', and began to sing it,

'Kookaburra sits on the old gum tree merry,
merry king of the bush is he.
Laugh, Kookaburra! Laugh, Kookaburra!
Gay your life must be.'

(Marion Sinclair 1932)

I repeated the first few lines several times and then triggered the (battery operated) call of the Kookaburra. The boy reached out to touch the Kookaburra very slowly and cautiously as if he thought it was alive and it might peck him! His fear was relieved as he made contact with the puppet and a smile slowly snuck onto his face. At that moment his world became a little less fearful, and a little more friendly.

Other small children were drawn to the distinctive call of the laughing Kookaburra. One baby carried by his very young mother, who herself was intrigued with the puppet, approached me. I motioned for her to take a seat and try on the puppet. With a beaming smile she accepted and began to entertain the baby. Within minutes a small group of boys and girls gathered around her and each time she spoke, in their familiar language, the children broke into bursts of laughter. She was a natural and had them all captivated.

ENTERTAINING THE CHILDREN

I moved through the chattering people, my eyes flitting around trying to take in all the activity, then finally they rested on a familiar face. It was my gracious husband, Greg. There he was sitting on a chair, surrounded by four or five children pressing in on him. A tiny toddler leaning on his lap with a deflated balloon in his hand, demanded Greg's attention to blow it up, while the other kids were bouncing their large inflated colourful balloons on his shoulders and back. I was touched to see the expression on his face, he looked totally engaged and like he was actually enjoying himself. I was amazed, as normally Greg has an irrational fear of sticky kids. He calls it, the 'Sticky Kids Syndrome.'

My gaze shifted to another scene, where a long skipping rope was being turned by two team members. Several kids were joyfully jumping in and out of the rope. Then the sound of some girls singing heartily drew my attention. They created a buzz of excitement which drew others in as their contagious laughter increased. A loudspeaker was in the process of being set up, and before long a type of Bollywood dance song was played at a loud volume. The girls knew every word of the song and clapped along, becoming even more excited. One by one the chairs were pushed aside, and the girls began to stand up and quite naturally they began to dance freely in a large circle. The circle quickly grew and without inhibition, the girls moved around in a circular motion, singing and dancing in their distinctive, almost choreographed Bollywood moves.

The joyful Bollywood display drew just about everyone to gather around them. The Nepalese girls had a beauty that appealed to the heart and mind, the sound of their lively, charismatic voices created so much laughter. Some, like me, could only observe on this stifling hot day, while others had the energy to actually join in. The clapping became louder and louder, and to my surprise, many of the girls in the team were irresistibly drawn in. They even had a go at the moves! Their courage, not knowing any of the words or the actions, was commendable. I was also amazed at their stamina to continue dancing, song-after-song for such a long time in the heat. The sweat rolled down their faces, but they continued regardless.

SERVING LUNCH UNDER THE MARQUEE

The dancing finally came to an end on the announcement that lunch was served, many were relieved. Lunch was an array of lavish and sumptuous Nepalese food, set out on a long table and served by the team. The feast, prepared by the chef and a small handful of his helpers, was amazing! It was enjoyed by all and devoured very quickly.

We gathered after lunch to hear a touching testimony of a young Nepalese lady who lived in the Centre we had come to serve. I admired her courage, as she was very young and had never spoken in public before. She nervously spoke from the heart (through a translator) and shared her very touching life story to total strangers. The young lady could not speak highly enough of all the help she had received from the Centre, and she gave all the glory to God for bringing her there.

A time of uplifting praise and worship with a short sermon from Randeep followed. Randeep spoke with passion, in a dialect which the local people understood and they were very quietly attentive to his every word. Next came a testament from one of the team members who shared her own heart wrenching account of how she came to know Jesus. I was touched by her sincerity and by the very difficult circumstances she shared.

Randeep then gave an altar call for anyone who wanted to accept Jesus into their life. I closed my eyes and with a tidal wave of compassion I began to pray in my heart for others. When I opened my eyes, I took a moment in that little green patch of heaven, I saw many young and old attendees gravitate towards the translators for prayer. Different groups of three or four huddled together and began to pray. I felt that same surge of compassion rise up and was stirred to raise my hands and continue praying. The divine presence of God filling the atmosphere was tangible on my fingertips. I felt like somehow, the spiritual had contacted the physical and an awesome fear of God washed over me. My heart was glad. I came away in awe and believing that the power of the Holy Spirit had fallen. Surely the prayers of His people were being answered!

Chapter Seven

DEPARTING KATHMANDU

17th October 2023

he same noise streaming through my window the previous night, was as loud as ever, but I was too tired for it to bother me. The early morning start seemed to have taken its toll on me, so much so that I began to wonder whether the benefit of getting up in the early hours was worth it. It wasn't even 9pm, yet I just couldn't stay awake. Before going to bed, I talked myself out of setting the alarm. After all, we had a big day ahead of us travelling on rough, potholed roads for a fair distance. That was all the rationale I needed. Before sleep took over, I prayed, confessing my weariness, asking God to wake me if he really wanted me to go to the prayer meeting. Within minutes I crashed!

The next morning, (17th) my eyes spontaneously sprang open and I felt so energised. Without hesitation I leaped out of bed and looked at the time, exactly three-forty-five in the morning. All I could say was, 'Thank you Lord, not just for waking me, but also for the feeling of boundless energy'. I chuckled when I donned my team T-shirt; it felt like my

'Superwoman' outfit! I had a remarkable spring in my step when I headed off to the prayer room. Greg was improving but still not one-hundred percent well; he remained asleep.

There were more souls in the room than in prior meetings. One young lady I noted, was already nursing a cup of coffee, like her life depended on it! Even though, it was good she was there. After prayer, Randeep read from a number of different scriptures, but the focus was on one verse from the book of Acts.

Peter replied, 'Each of you must repent of your sins and turn to God, and be baptised in the name of Jesus Christ for the forgiveness of your sins. Then you will receive the gift of the Holy Spirit.'

(Acts 2:38).

It is almost impossible to capture and reiterate all that was said however it was good and made a lot of sense. What I took away, were two things. Firstly, the simplicity that is in Christ. What God requires of us is not at all complicated, in fact it seems too easy to be true. We just have to read those words in Acts 2:38 and then apply them.

Until we repent of ours sins and turn to God, we are drowning in our own sin. Dealing with sin in our life is a losing battle, we struggle desperately trying to be that, 'good person' we want to be, however we don't have any power over sin and we can't save ourselves. Without the gift of Salvation and the Holy Spirit, we will eventually go under and drown. All we can do, is to bring our sinful, unworthy selves to God, just as we are, and He does the rest.

What a relief to be reminded of this! The battle is no

longer ours. It's all about what Christ did for us, not what we can do in our own efforts. The day I surrendered my life to God, in humility, was the day when I first realised this truth, but hearing it again, this time, I knew and understood it more fully.

Secondly, I was reminded that we can fully rely on Jesus for everything. As believers we have the gift of the Holy Spirit, we know that Jesus is the healer of every disease and sickness, so we can fully rely on Jesus for healing of any kind. We must not and cannot assume that we have the gift of healing, it's all about Him not us. Therefore, if healing does not take place, it doesn't mean that we have failed, nor does it mean that God has failed. Rather, we are to remember that our God is sovereign. We can't and shouldn't try to understand the 'why's and why-nots.

> *'Trust in the lord with all your heart; do not depend on your own understanding.'*
>
> *(Proverbs 3:5).*

> *'My thoughts are nothing like your thoughts,' says the Lord, 'And my ways are far beyond anything you could imagine.'*
>
> *(Isaiah 55:8).*

It's always His will, not ours. We simply need to yield and let God be God.

The session ended by praying for one another. It was still dark outside with not a soul stirring. Greg was sleeping when I returned to the room and there was still a short interval before meeting up with Elizabeth, so I had some time to reflect. My mind replayed the teaching session before it wandered on to other things. Then the pre-readings came to mind. In preparation for the trip, we were encouraged to gain some understanding of the historical aspect of Nepal as well as the world of Hinduism and Buddhism. The readings were insightful and helped me to understand a little more about the culture before actually stepping into it. A stimulating topic which intrigued me was the caste system. I discovered that it's based on Hinduism and it's probably the biggest hindrance to the social development of Nepali society. The system is divided into four main social classes. The Brahmin caste, seen as the highest caste, are rulers of all parts of society. The Sudra is seen as the lowest caste and are subject to the most isolation and discrimination in society. Kshatriya and Vaishya are somewhere in between. It's a known fact that the lower caste people accept Jesus more readily than the higher caste people because they find that, in God's eyes, they are all equal (Gellner, 2007).

I learnt that Nepal is a diversely multicultural country with 123 languages, 131 ethnic groups and many religious groups, with only 1.4% of the total population being Christian. The rest of the population comprises 82.3% Hindu. Hinduism is a polytheistic religion with belief in many gods and goddesses, it's not really concerned with one's salvation and eternal life. With 9.0% being Buddhist whose belief is in Karma and ritual practices, 4.3% Muslim and only 3.0% Kirat.

Although Christianity was introduced into Nepal as early as 1628 by the Jesuit priests, they did not stay very long. Nepal remained a Hindu kingdom formed by the expansion of the Gorkha Kingdom which lasted until a civil uprising in 1950, where a parliamentary democracy was established under a constitution rather than an absolute monarchy. Again, the period of parliamentary rule didn't last very long; it came to an end following a coup in 1960. Political parties were banned and the power was placed back into the hands of the monarch, known as the Panchayat System (Schmidt, 20 May 2015, p. 47).

Thirty years later, in 1996 the Maoist Communist armed forces started a civil war. This hindered the evangelistic work to spread the Gospel in the rural areas and stunted the growth of Christianity. It wasn't until 2007, when the war ended, that new hope for everyone, including Nepali Christians, returned. In that same year, Nepal was declared a secular state, and guaranteed the rights of citizens to profess, practice, and preserve their religion, social order, or cultural tradition. The catch was that the Constitution also completely prohibited the conversion from one religion to another religion. In reality, it only guaranteed the right to profess and practice one's own religion insofar as it is done without infringement upon the religion of another.

The constitution of Nepal today declares that every person shall have the freedom to profess and practice his/her own religion, however bans on proselytisation still exist. Democracy is still not applied freely in Nepal, as this prohibition of conversion actually prevents the right to practice the religion of choice.

According to the Asia Missions Association it is apparent that the definition of secularism in Nepal is biased against Christians and other religious minorities, and it protects and promotes the Hindu religion and alienates other faiths (Koirala, 2018). The primary accusations against Christians in Nepali society are that they are religion changers and culture destroyers. The local police and lower courts often misinterpret laws to punish religious individuals for living out their faith. The right to freedom of religion therefore is limited in Nepal due to the bias against Christian believers and other religious minorities.

In spite of the limitations, the Good News is spreading effectively in Nepal, even into the remote areas. God is doing amazing work through many Christian organisations which engage with the newly formed Nepali churches. Both the organisations and the local churches have been actively working together, not only in word but also in action. The churches, by being salt and light through witnessing to the local community, and, the Christian organisations (i.e. Impact Nations) by engaging closely with the provision of medical clinics, clean water filters, valuable support and encouragement to new believers and upcoming pastors.

Also, in the remote areas, the number of small churches has grown due to the provision of funds for their construction. In these modest churches, many people are coming to Christ as a result of the Gospel being proclaimed by word, practised by action and demonstrated by life. A classic example of this kind of engagement was clearly demonstrated when Christian organisations and Nepali churches worked together in response to the devastating earthquake of 2015. Afterwards many souls were added to the kingdom. Where there is unity, the result is always the same… souls are added! (International Centre for Law and Religion Studies)

Elizabeth and I began another power walk through the streets of Thamel, but this time we were better able to find our way around in, what seemed to us, more familiar sights and sounds. I was amazed that nobody else showed an interest in joining us and felt that they were missing out, big time. Praying as we walked and pondering over the insightful teachings from Randeep seemed to strengthen and consolidate our understanding. In fact, just being the two of us turned out to be good; we were able to share a little of life at a deeper level and I got to know Elizabeth much better. We were both Registered Nurses excited about the prospect of working in the remote clinic during the JOC. Our walk ended much quicker that day, as we were becoming more familiar with the streets. We made it back well in time to enjoy an amazing breakfast feast.

As our feasting came to a close, we were drawn to the sound of melodious voices and well-tuned guitar strings. Excitement filled the back of the dining room space as we joined the quickly growing circle of people. Hands were lifted up in praise to our God and voices echoed expressions of adoration and worship. The volume grew louder and stronger as more entered into the worship and yet we became as one voice united by love for the Father. For a moment, conscious of God's presence, I stopped singing and remained still, just wanting to soak up His presence without uttering a word. My natural response to this encounter was an overwhelming feeling of gratitude to God. The connection seemed strong and even palpable through my fingertips and the palms of my raised hands. I felt a stirring of the spirit within and all I wanted to do was to give my total self to Him. Momentarily it felt like there was no one else in the room. I was captivated in a wonderful, glorious encounter and began to praise and worship with all my heart. How can mere words describe a divine encounter with the living God? They cannot!

In my home church our worship together is not like this. It's all so very structured. Nearly everyone around me seems to be inhibited and reluctant to even raise their hands. We are told when to stand, when to sit, and are not given any opportunity for spontaneous expressions of worship. Our time of worship is scheduled and cannot go beyond the allotted time slot. As soon as the last song is finished, we are asked to be seated. Sometimes, when I feel God's presence, my heart is pounding and all I want to do is to continue worshipping. The abrupt end to our worship is devastating to me. I feel so restricted and am unable to give my total self in worship.

I do believe that worship is a lifestyle, it can be done at any time, any day of the week, and in many different ways. We all deeply love and treasure God, so I don't believe that worship is a task just for the music team alone. When I reflect on the character of God and His perfect holiness, I feel that the only posture to worship God is to bow in humility and reverence. I know that I am far from His character, but I also know and thank God that the moment I repented and turned to him, I was made righteous in Him. I have received God's spirit and I am justified in His sight. His spirit in me affirms that I am His child.

And Christ lives within you, so even though your body will die because of sin, the Spirit gives you life because you have been made right with God.

(Romans 8:10).

So, you have not received a spirit that makes you fearful slaves. Instead, you received God's Spirit when he adopted you as his own children. Now we call him, "Abba, Father."

(Romans 8:15).

Therefore, there is now no condemnation for those who are in Christ Jesus.

(Romans 8:1).

In John Piper's bestselling book, *Let the Nations Be Glad*, he writes about worship and he implies that mission is the servant of worship. This is how he puts it in his opening chapter,

'Missions exists because worship doesn't ... worship, therefore, is the goal of missions.' (17).

I do like Piper's emphasis that, 'The chief end of man is to glorify God *by* enjoying Him forever.' Piper suggests that, we most definitely can have full access to God. The purpose of evangelising is so that man, in his sinful nature, can be cleansed by Christ's redeeming work, and, be made holy, therefore able to approach the very throne room of God (Piper, 1993).

It goes without saying that we need humility and reverence before a holy God, and we need to grow a posture of dying to self, daily, to achieve this. That said, the scriptures also, tell us ...

True worshipers will worship the Father in spirit and in truth. The father is looking for those who will worship him that way.

(John 4:23b).

Chapter Eight

CHITWAN

17th October 2023

*A*fter a jam-packed morning that began with a prayer/teaching session, then the prayer walk with Elizabeth, followed by breakfast and a motivating interlude of worship, the time had finally come for us to leave Kathmandu. Our bags were packed and loaded onto the roof racks of one large coach, the ginger tablets were being handed out, and we were more than ready to begin our journey to the subtropical climate of Chitwan.

The plan was to pay a short visit to a social enterprise and stop for lunch before embarking on the six-hour drive to Chitwan. The social enterprise that we visited, cannot be mentioned by name (for reasons of confidentiality) but will be referred to as the Centre. The Centre was created to strengthen young women in the face of poverty, social injustice and other cultural attitudes against women pursuing their dreams. This was achieved through the provision of an internship program where young women could enrol and bring their gifts and talents to the Centre. Here they could be encouraged and equipped to grow in their personal development and other professional skills. As a result of the internship, many young ladies had become more resilient and were empowered to find employment or inspired to start a small business of their own.

On the tour around the Centre, we actually met a couple of the women who were growing their entrepreneurial dreams in the form of a small business. One young lady was an extremely gifted artist who seemed almost embarrassed when she was encouraged to display her repertoire of amazing paintings. She was a beautiful, petite young woman with straight black hair tied up in a long ponytail. She seemed a little shell-shocked and lacking in confidence as she turned the pages of her large sketch book. We were a crowd of total strangers to her, and by the look on her face she must have felt quite intimidated. Her expression was serious, perhaps even fearful, as she stood barely taller than those sitting down. This budding artist wore a loose yellow T-shirt over loose-fitting blue jeans which made her look even more diminutive. This nervous young lady seemed to be overwhelmed, apart from a shy whisper of a smile, she really didn't know how to respond when people complimented her artwork. Then, when someone bought one of her paintings on the spot and tried to hand over the US dollars, she shook her head and refused to take the cash. When it was pressed into her hand, immediately, as though it were a hot potato, she passed the cash over to Randeep. He, in turn handed the money straight back to her and told her it was hers. At that she almost cried in disbelief. She had no idea of the value of her paintings. This experience gave her a huge boost of confidence. By the time she had shown all of her paintings, the young lady had sold several of them. With each sale, her self-esteem grew. The shy smile also grew bigger and bigger, until she was beaming with delight. She was so appreciative and it really showed.

The Centre was improving the lives of many young women like this young artist. In practical ways the girls were being helped with marketing strategies and were given other opportunities to become known, but more importantly, the girls began to realise their true worth through acceptance and encouragement. Many were perusing their dreams, fulfilling their potential and succeeding.

There were other young ladies who we met that day, one of which had begun a startup company called, 'Apple World.' She manufactured apple cider and other apple-based products, as well as macramé products which she made and sold.

GIRL DISPLAYING HER PAINTINGS

For me, the visit to the Centre was truly a meaningful and rewarding experience. I was acutely aware of the similarities of these young Nepalese girls to the Latino girls I had worked with in Peru. Deep, sad emotions were triggered during the visit, as I remembered how certain young girls, who, through no fault of their own, had suffered abuse and were victims of exploitation. The sadness I felt lingered only for a moment as I began to recall the many success stories too. In Peru many young girls were set free from the chains of poverty and depravation, through education and similar opportunities as were being provided at the Centre. I recalled this scripture ... and was left with a lighter heart.

God's law was given so that all people could see how sinful they were. But as people sinned more and more, God's wonderful grace became more abundant.

(Romans 5:20).

The tour around the centre took a lot longer than planned so we ended up setting off much later than anticipated. Also, our extended lunch break added to the delay. The day before we had messaged through our, thirty-one lunch orders to save time. From the moment we arrived at the Café, it was mayhem. The place was crowded with people and our order wasn't even near completion. The Café Bethesda, was a local business which the Centre supported, so we simply waited patiently.

Chitwan district is located in the subtropical lowlands at the foot of the Himalayas. The journey from Kathmandu to Chitwan used to be an arduous trek, only reached by foot, which took several weeks in the 1950's. Today, our drive took six hours in an airconditioned coach. Although that sounds like a breeze… it wasn't!

I nearly jumped out of my skin the first time our driver thumped on his air horn. He did this repeatedly, in fact, on approach to every single curve in the long, convoluting road. At times, there were very scary moments. The road became a very narrow dirt road causing the driver to scrape dangerously close to the cliff edge in some places. Once, where the road narrowed into one single lane for both sides, I could see another vehicle approaching. We were on a head-on collision course, and our driver continued, hardly slowing down, but instead, blasting his air horn extremely long and loud. I closed my eyes and prayed. When I opened them, the vehicle in front of us was backing up and our driver was moving towards him in a very intimidating way. After a distance of doing this, the other vehicle eventually found a space, only just wide enough, for our coach to squeeze past him. It was a nightmare!

We were jolted and knocked about on the rough potholes, for most of the trip so much so, that all of us who had neck pillows pulled them out of our packs and put them to use. Although the cushioning effect helped immensely, it was still impossible to relax. I found myself closing my eyes on several occasions…but not to sleep!

The weather in the second half of October is supposed to be a little cooler but it seemed hotter and more humid than ever. It all became rather oppressive and unbearable when the aircon. could barely deal with the extreme heat and humidity.

Arriving in Chitwan's town centre, was the highlight of the whole trip. Amazingly, out of nowhere, a huge elephant walked alongside our coach. It sauntered slowly with the traffic down the main street in the centre of town. This magnificent creature seemed inquisitive; its huge, single eye peered through the window, as if it was looking at me. I was excited to see such a spectacle. Through an open window I reached out and managed to touch its thick, coarse skin just for a moment. I looked up at the owner, sitting bareback, high above, just behind the elephants' enormous ears. He appeared oblivious to our coach as we moved in unison. Although slow, it was busy; the road was wider than usual with two broad lanes, one for each direction. Both lanes were full of motorbikes and people competing with the token Mahindra. Despite that amazing experience, the best part of the whole drive was that it was finally over!

The temperature was dropping and the heat was more bearable as we spilled out of the coach. It was probably around twenty-seven degrees. The sky was clear and the land was still moist, making everything glisten in beautiful shades of lush green. October, just after the monsoon, is the best time to visit Nepal, for many reasons, trekking being one.

We all piled into the large air-conditioned foyer of our hotel where we were warmly greeted by a young Nepalese waiter, who approached with a tray full of chilled glasses of fruit juice. The refreshing welcome and the pleasant surroundings created a hum of excitement among the team. We were blown away by the quality of the hotel. On entering our room, a large comfortable, air-conditioned space with a sofa, queen bed and T.V. lay before us. Greg and I couldn't believe our eyes. Instinctively, I flopped on the bed which was wonderfully soft and comfortable compared to our bed in the previous hotel. Greg checked out the bathroom and gave the thumbs up. This was definitely an upgrade on Kathmandu, probably a five-star hotel. Needless to say, no one complained or needed a room change.

Arriving later than predicted, a change of plan was necessary. The visit to the remote village had to be postponed until the following day. One thing we learned very quickly during this Journey of Compassion, was that plans change rapidly, and everything takes longer than you think! I've experienced this before and I'm beginning to think that mission trips are often as much about teaching us patience and slowing us down to become less task orientated and more people focused.

After a wonderful dinner we regrouped for a debriefing session followed by the sorting of medications. We were given an invitation to attend the prayer time again at 4am each morning, and we finished off with a time of worship together. Free time was then given for us to rest up in preparation for the busy day ahead. However, a rumour that there was a rhinoceros wandering down the main street had been spread and a group of excited thrill-seeking adventurers decided to check it out. At least about eight of us headed out to see if we could spot the rhino before going to bed. By then it was dark, but many of the restaurants were lit up like Christmas trees, it seemed safe enough. After walking a fair distance, we decided that the rhino was probably not going to show. Most of the group stopped at a coffee shop, while Greg and I broke off to seek out the popular, 'Momos,' our favourite savoury snack.

On return to the hotel, we heard that the rumour was in fact true. The rhino did appear, slowly trotting right passed the coffee shop where we left the group. A handful from the group, told us that they had separated and followed the rhino everywhere it went. We didn't believe them at first, but they took great joy in showing us multiple photos to prove it. The rhino seemed as though at home, not in the least disturbed by people. One of the residents commented that, 'The rhino thinks humans are crazy for building a road right through its territory!' I'm sure that must be exactly how it felt. Greg and I missed out big time on the rhino… but the Momo's were worth it!

That night we finally got to sleep quite late. I set my alarm for 3.45am, not wanting to miss out on, what I considered the most valuable part of the day, the prayer session. I happened to wake up five minutes before my alarm went off, and to my delight, despite the short few hours' sleep, I felt energised and ready to roll. Greg, on the other hand, rolled over in a semi-conscious state, inhaling noisily, while I breathed a quiet sigh of relief that I hadn't disturbed him. Greg was almost fully recovered but wisely decided to go easy on himself.

Chapter Nine

A CALL TO INTIMACY WITH GOD

18th October 2023

*J*ust as I got to the prayer session, others were arriving at the same time. I struggled to hide my amusement at the sight of the motley bunch gathered before me (me included). Yet, there we were, in all our human frailties and limitations, hungry and ready to consume the word of God and hear from our creator, through Randeep. No earthly pleasure could stand in the way of our being in God's presence, even just for a moment. Unfortunately, there were many in the team who were suffering with, 'Delhi-belli,' which prevented them from attending.

As always, after the exchange of some short pleasantries, Randeep, in his unassuming way, suggested that we begin with prayer. We bowed our heads in silent pause, and as he proceeded in the quiet stillness, his softly spoken words made the early hours seem very sacred and soul-enriching. When Randeep prayed for those who were unwell, occasional whisper's, 'Yes Lord,' and 'Amen,' could be heard echoing from sincere hearts. We knew that we were all in agreement. Our love for God and others, was without question unanimous, and we could feel the warmth of His presence fill that space. It never ceases to amaze me that God makes Himself known to us in that way. For me, the effect is always the same, it's a sense of being exquisitely recharged with a boost of joy, peace and positive energy.

The main content of Randeep's prayer was simply the worship of God and the recognition of His holiness. The only requests made, were that God would give us wisdom and discernment to understand the word that we were about to read, and that He would move mightily in His power on our behalf as we shared our faith with others. We each then read a verse from the scriptures, beginning with the book of Acts.

Among the prophets and teachers of the church at Antioch of Syria were Barnabas, Simeon (called "the black man"), Lucius (from Cyrene), Manaen (the childhood companion of King Herod Antipas), and Saul. 2 One day as these men were worshiping the Lord and fasting, the Holy Spirit said, 'Appoint Barnabas and Saul for the special work to which I have called them.' 3 So after more fasting and prayer, the men laid their hands on them and sent them on their way.

(Acts 13:1-3).

The next reading was,

Greet Rufus, whom the Lord picked out to be his very own; and also, his dear mother, who has been a mother to me.

(Romans 16:13).

The final reading from *Mark,*

'A passerby named Simon, who was from Cyrene, was coming in from the countryside just then, and the soldiers forced him to carry Jesus' cross. (Simon was the father of Alexander and Rufus).

(Mark 15:21).

Reiterated in my own words, these verses tell us that the Holy Spirit instructed some prophets and teachers while they were fasting and worshipping the Lord. The Holy Spirit told them to set apart Barnabas and Saul for a special work to which God had called them. The men (after more prayer and fasting) laid their hands on Barnabas and Saul and sent them on their way. Also, we are told that Rufus was picked out by the Lord to be his very own and that Simon from Cyrene just happened to be passing by from the countryside when he was forced, by the soldiers, to carry Jesus' cross.

Randeep made it clear that God calls all of us to be His very own, and that He has a special work for every one of us. We can and will discover what God's calling is on our life, if we seek intimacy with Him. He explained that even Simon, the foreigner passing by, is a picture of being snatched into service and discipleship by God. If He should so desire God can do the same with any one of us. The scriptures pointed to, 'a calling to intimacy with God.' The emphasis being on seeking after God. That is, seriously seeking with a hunger and a thirst for an intimate relationship with Him. Worship and fasting being of paramount importance if we are to be set apart and led by the Holy Spirit.

At the close of the session, we all dispersed without a word spoken. Instead of heading back to my room, I stepped outside into the tranquillity of the Hotel gardens and walked along the pavers towards the river. It was still dark, apart from the stars and the moon illuminating the sky. The celestial lights provided an awesome and faint reflection on the water. The grass glistened in places, wet from the rain during the night. Alone in my thoughts and inspired by the teaching, all I wanted to do was to maintain a state of worship and continue quietly listening and sensing His majestic presence. It had been some time since I had felt this close to God. In my silent reverie I soaked up the strength of the stillness surrounding me. Only the odd sound of a bird's call broke the silence. I was in a good place, a place where I felt loved, where I felt as though I really was His very own.

This awesome interlude with God came to an abrupt finish by the sensation of my mobile vibrating in my pocket; it was time to meet up with Eizabeth. We met in the foyer and with a bounce in our step we set out for our prayer walk, just before dawn. Elizabeth seemed as encouraged as I was about the teaching session; we were both eager to seek God more and more. We headed down the main street talking and praying as we walked. I felt that there was no stopping us. We were really in the flow of what God was doing, and we knew that there was much to pray for with our first clinic day about to start.

We were mindful of the fact that we were entering into a battle of spiritual warfare and that there was much opposition. Our response to that was to prepare ourselves with the full armour of God. We acknowledged our need for God and that we could do nothing in and of ourselves. We covered so much ground, in a spiritual sense, and yet we had probably walked only one kilometre.

On reaching the T-junction at the very end of the street, close to the same river, we did a left turn into a minor street. To our surprise we were immediately faced with two ginormous elephants approaching us from the opposite direction. Elizabeth let out a shriek of delight... 'Oh my God, I love elephants!' she exclaimed, in a typical American way. Her pace picked up as she headed towards them. We were very much distracted from anything spiritual from that moment. As the elephants moved closer, I felt a little uneasy by their sheer supremacy, but Elizabeth was obviously loving every moment of it; she allowed one of the elephants to sniff and touch her with its trunk and she responded with friendly cuddles. Elizabeth was all over it, she just couldn't get enough. I on the other hand, kept my distance to prevent the elephant's trunk from getting too close, I was a little overwhelmed by the enormity of their size.

One of the owners, sitting comfortably bareback on his elephant, must have noticed that I was reticent and assured me that his elephant was tame and harmless. The other owner suggested that, if we had any notes to offer the elephant, it would take the Rupees from our hand. I happened to have a few small notes in my pocket and began to roll them up, but before I had finished, the elephant snatched the cash right out of my hand, quite forcefully with its trunk. I jumped with fright! The elephant then lifted its trunk above his head towards the owner, who promptly received the notes with much appreciation and a toothless smile. It was hard for Elizabeth to break away; she caressed and kissed the elephants inquiring about their names. I took lots of photos and after lingering for a while we headed back to the hotel at lightning speed.

We made it back, just in the nick of time. While talking with others over breakfast, Greg and I learnt that there had been a heavy storm which raged all through the latter part of the night. Many had had a rude awakening by loud claps of thunder and lightning but surprisingly, we had slept through it all!

The worship that followed, was so powerful and edifying. We prayed for each other before we set off on (for many of us) our first encounter with a 'least-reached people group.' We made sure that the remote village was also covered by a powerful mantle of prayer.

Chapter Ten

FIRST REMOTE VILLAGE

18th October 2023 (continued)

The village was another forty-five minute drive further out from the centre of Chitwan. The people inhabiting this village, and most of the other remote villages, were predominantly Hindu farmers. Buddhism is practiced to a lesser extent and both faiths lived peaceably, side by side, in some cases even sharing the same temple. The farmers work in the maize, rice and wheat fields. Chitwan is known to be the major maize producing area in Nepal, but on a smaller scale, they cultivate beans, mustard, vegetables and bananas.

The sky was clear and blue on this gloriously sunny morning and already the temperature was touching on twenty-six degrees, so it was going to be a scorcher of a day. Once the coach was loaded with medical supplies, water filters and crates of bottled water, the precious yet motley bunch all piled in, followed by the smart looking Nepali translators. We set off and were soon zig-zagging up a mountain to the melodious sound of Randeep playing his guitar. We attempted to sing-along as others began to sing but it was too difficult to compete with the sound of the deafening blasts of the airhorn. I soon gave up singing, but the diehards continued despite the challenge of the horn and being jerked about over the rough, weather-beaten terrain.

The ever-changing window views kept me occupied for most of the trip. We passed abundant green vegetation, growing luxuriantly on the flat terraces carved into the side of the mountain. The green and yellow crops were framed like a painting by taller trees bunched neatly around their perimeters. The darker green banana trees made it all look so picturesque. In one corner of the terraces, I caught sight of a compact little group of small dwellings with corrugated metal roofs, supported by walls made of some kind of rendered plaster. The walls were painted mainly white. The tin roofs were held precariously in situ by large rocks randomly placed on the top. Occasionally we passed other dwellings which were more ornately decorated with bright coloured paint, mosaic tiled walls and sturdy roof tiles.

One of the many different sights along the way were the outdoor communal showers, usually situated in front of a small group of dwellings, where they were obviously shared. I wondered how the shy Nepalese people could possibly shower in public, until I saw one in use. They showered partially dressed, the ladies in a wrap-around cloth and the men in their underpants.

OUTDOOR COMMUNAL SHOWER

Most of the showers had a simple hose dangling down with no shower head attached. The hose was nearly always left running with a stream of water constantly leaking out onto the concrete slab at the base. I was curious to know why the hose always seemed to be leaking. (and taps in the kitchens were nearly always dripping).

Apparently, this cultural habit of allowing the water to trickle and drip away was based on the belief that the water would flow all the way back to its original source and it was therefore not wasted. With the abundance of fast

flowing rivers all over Nepal this was probably a reasonable assumption.

Another fascinating sight was, what appeared to be, the
many, very tall, golden/brownish coloured haystacks. These
tall structures of varying shapes, scattered along the edge of
the fields turned out to be made of rice straw rather than
hay. They appeared like sculptures created around a tree
branch with a plastic bag attached to the top, the purpose of
which I am uncertain.

The bus finally arrived and we were greeted by an
excited crowd of men, women and children. The men who
dressed in simple T-shirts and jeans, were outnumbered by
the throng of petite Nepalese women wrapped in beautiful
vibrant colours.

Just a few men wore the traditional dress known as the
'suruwal,' which is loose-fitting trousers and a long, knee-
length shirt. Both are typically white. The suruwal is worn
with a 'Topi,' which looks like a type of skullcap with an
unusual boat-like shape. The traditional dress can vary in
style and colour according to each different ethnic community, but the Topi is the same among all groups as it was
originally created to unite the many different ethnic groups
in the country. The Topi has now become a symbol of
Nepal.

Many of the women wore long-sleeved, knee-length
blouses with either a long skirt or baggy pants, (known as
the Gunyo Cholo) some of which were of solid colours of
saffron, scarlet, emerald, pink and royal blue, others, of
patterns and printed fabric.

The women also covered their heads with a large,
matching chiffon or cotton scarf, which in some cases was
elegantly draped over the body instead of the head. The

Sari, another traditional garment was not worn, this is mainly preserved for special celebrations.

The women in their colourful garments and beautiful white smiles, seem shy and timid, yet the adorning of make-up was widespread and popular. Even the way they neatly tied back their hair, spoke of the meticulous care and attention paid to their appearance. The ladies nearly always had long jet black hair, wrapped in forms of impressive spiral twists and knots.

In spite of belonging to an underprivileged community and living without the basics, these Nepalese people seemed to exude a sense of cultural pride in themselves, unlike anything I've witnessed before. When I think of the poorest, roughest suburbs in my country, or in England or Ireland for that matter, the culture is lacking in self-pride, and even in respect towards one another.

Here it was different. It was like a kind of sacred dignity in both the men and the women. I was taken aback by how readily they showed respect toward each other and towards outsiders too.

The children dressed and played and laughed pretty much like any children the world over, but they were charmingly different too. They were very inclusive of each other; no child was left playing alone. In the way they greeted me, that same undeniable, captivating respect beamed out of them. It was in their DNA. Their enthusiasm to make contact, (without asking for money) made me feel valued. This warmth and enthusiasm, not only towards me and other adults, but also towards their peers. How wonderful! I felt we could do with taking a page out of their cultural book.

After the initial welcome, we walked over a grassy

square patch under the relieving shade of a saffron coloured canopy. We walked towards a building which was used as a meeting place for just about everything. A few steps led up into a large hall with an 'A' frame roof.

Inside the building, at the far end of the hall, was a small stage, elevated about half a metre off the timber floor. To the left of the stage was a wooden pulpit with two small vases of red flowers placed on it, attached to its front was a white cross. Church meetings were obviously held here although there were no chairs in sight.

On the back wall, behind the pulpit, hung some heavy red velvet curtains, which extended across the whole stage. The many open windows along each side of the hall together with the ceiling fans brought little relief from the heat.

The hall was empty apart from the two long tables that had already been set up with a variety of medical equipment. The medical team who had arrived first, were in the process of setting up another two tables for the pharmacy area. The long tables were placed end-to-end to form one long table across the front of the stage. On these tables, laid out in an organised fashion, were vast amounts of various medications, ointments, vitamins and sunglasses.

The Clinic Coordinator, Genevieve, had been on several similar JOC trips overseeing everything and anything to do with the medical team. Genevieve, a middle-aged woman, with a light-weight small frame darted around the hall like a whirlwind. Her thick brown eyebrows matched the colour of her long straight hair, which was mostly tied back in a hair clip or bun.

As I entered the hall, I noticed the expression on Genevieve's face displayed a degree of stress I had not seen there during orientation. Ordinarily, Genevieve was quite laid back with a witty sense of humour and a wide teeth-showing smile. I had thought that she was unfazed by anything, but being bombarded with questions from every direction wasn't easy. It seemed like everyone wanted a piece of her, including Lesley and me.

After consulting with Genevieve, we gravitated toward our allocated table and began to check the equipment and familiarise ourselves with the clinic's routine. Lesley and I had only met a few weeks prior to the trip, in a group who all happened to live in the same suburb. Because this was my first trip, I was to work alongside Lesley, a doctor and a seasoned team member, who had also done many trips over the years. Lesley was a gently spoken, mature lady with short white, wavy hair. She was a great communicator with a calm air about her and I was keen to work with her. Just as the clinic was about to commence, however, Genevieve approached and in her efficient voice said, 'There's an extra translator available if you feel confident enough to work on your own.' I responded, 'I'm not super confident, but I'm willing to give it a go, so long as I can refer to a doctor if needed.' It was agreed, so I began to set up my end of the table.

Soon enough, I was approached by an adolescent Nepali boy with a winning smile, who introduced himself, 'I am Basanta Pahari, your translator for today.' Although he did have an obvious Nepali accent, his well-spoken English was clear and easy to understand. I was surprised that he spoke so well because he looked so young, perhaps only fifteen years old. His olive skin was clear and smooth; not a wrinkle to be seen. Although Basanta had some typical Nepali facial features, almond-shaped eyes and dark bushy eyebrows, at around 5ft 8 inches tall, he was taller than the average Nepali man. He could have easily been mistaken for a Latino boy.

BASANTA & BRIDGET

After some polite conversation getting to know each other, I perceived that Basanta was a very good-natured and inquisitive young man with a willingness to listen intently. His exceptionally mature manner, didn't match his baby-faced impression, and curiosity got the better of me; I was compelled to ask, 'How old are you Basanta?'

'Seventeen,' he said, 'I'm just finishing high school,' he exclaimed with a big sunny smile. And still no wrinkles! Basanta continued, 'I'm hoping to do further studies, when school is out'. Just then, an elderly lady was escorted to our table by Beck, one of the runners, and our full attention was taken by her.

I found conversing through a translator quite chal-lenging at first, because I instinctively made eye contact with the woman and automatically began to speak directly to her. Then after speaking a few sentences, I suddenly realised that she had no idea what I was saying. When the penny dropped, all three of us laughed. I embarrassed myself by repeating this at least three more times before I got the hang of it. It's so unnatural not to look at the person you are speaking to.

Sure enough, our first patient turned out to have a complicated condition, she needed help and I was dubious of what to do. Everyone was super busy, so we had to wait. After a short time, Lesley became free and I quickly grabbed her attention, before she went on to the next patient. It turned out that the lady had a long-term, chronic complaint, which Lesley found to be quite complex, and she too referred to a second doctor.

Initially, I had the tendency to refer patients too readily, but after a short time, my confidence grew and my nursing skills from way back kicked in. With each patient I began to relax a little more and I managed to deal with most of the cases myself. That's when I began to enjoy the experience of helping others.

At one point, in between patients, despite being busy, I stopped for a moment to rehydrate and went to a nearby window for fresh air. Just outside, I could see some children gathered around the open window, peeping into the hall with a curious sparkle in their eyes. They were so excited to see all the action. Joy just filled my heart at the sight.

CURIOUS KIDS PEERING IN THE WINDOW

By the open front doorway of the clinic, I got a glimpse of Iana, a team member who, in spite of her swollen sore foot, became the first line of contact for every person who attended the clinic that day. She did this by hobbling her way to a table and sitting, with her painful foot elevated on a chair. On arrival to Nepal, Iana had had the misfortune of being bitten by a spider, but she rarely complained, instead she just got on with the job and worked hard and efficiently most of the day. With the help of a translator, Iana communicated with each one of the patient's filling out their details on the white Registration Cards and informing them of the next step. By her side was Marcel, her devoted husband who helped her whenever she needed anything. Iana was a very sociable and relatable person whose words just rolled off her tongue in a soft, gentle Canadian accent which was so pleasant on the ears.

A couple of runners directed the crowds of people here and there. Many more patients filled the hall, some sitting at each of the five different stations, some with extended family standing around them, observing intently. At the pharmacy table, men and women occupied all the chairs while others were standing in wait. Those who had requested prayer were being escorted by a runner, through the exit door at the back of the hall and were taken to the prayer team outside. All in all the clinic was an awesome sight of activity and so incredibly enriching to see.

Basanta and I continued to work smoothly together until the lunch break was announced. We dealt with an array of cases, some quite challenging, but Basanta managed to translate really well, and I felt so accomplished making my own decisions and taking accountability for myself. Even when I couldn't help several people with chronic problems, I discovered that most of the time, they were happy to be directed to the prayer team. The Nepalese people were a people well familiar with prayer. This being obvious by the large numbers who accepted the invite, and by the incredible amount of gratitude they expressed at the suggestion.

Just outside the clinic building was another beehive of activity where many children were being entertained with craft and bubble blowing. Water filters were being demon-strated to the locals and food had been prepared by the chef and set out ready to serve. After such a full morning we were all well and truly ready for something to eat.

TEAM SERVING LUNCH

It was a very busy place after lunch too, beginning with a time of worship when Isaiah and his wife Prathna began to strum their guitars and sing. The area where they stood, just in front of the hall, at the top of the few steps, transformed into a stage, since it was raised above ground level. Everyone else was standing at the bottom of the steps including the rest of the team.

First, we joined in with singing, then the Nepalese women began clapping and dancing with joy. The delightful sound continued for a while, until it came to a time of sharing. On the quasi stage, various team members shared a bible story or a testimony, while many of the Nepali people stood listening. At the same time, others in the team, set up rows of chairs at ground level. By the time it came for Adam, the youth pastor in our team, to speak, the chairs were fully occupied by the women, some with children sitting on their knees. Most of the men stood around the perimeter of the area behind the chairs.

A TIME TO WORSHIP

Adam spoke clearly and hardly needed a microphone as he was able to project his voice very well. He was a robust young man, with a short back and sides haircut that matched his full black beard and moustache. Adam had an amusing, contagious laugh and was always ready to create a bit of fun; he was also a very authentic guy with a serious side. He shared the Gospel that morning, to a captive audience and when he had finished, he invited the team to find a translator and pray for someone. Greg and I quickly spotted two young ladies, the one who was wearing an I.D. badge was obviously a translator looking for someone to pray. Before we approached, we quickly prayed and asked God to give us the right words, and off we went. We were pretty green and a little nervous; the prospect of praying for healing and expecting to see instant answers was like stepping out into the great unknown. I had mixed feelings of excitement and apprehension. Before long, people were being prayed for in little clusters of three or four.

On greeting the two young women, we introduced ourselves and straight away the translator told us that the young lady was a Christian. I began by asking her name and finding out what she wanted us to pray for. Rita, the young woman, was simply requesting prayer for her unsaved family. We listened intently as she spoke through the translator. Apparently, Rita had decided to follow Jesus several years ago when Impact Nations had made their first trip into the village, but she was still the only member of her family who knew Jesus. After a moment of silence, I invited the Holy Spirit into the situation and asked for guidance. When I felt to pray, I gave thanks for Rita's faithfulness and acknowledged God's love over her and her family. After a short pause, Greg prayed for a breakthrough, for the salvation of her husband, her two young children, her siblings and her parents. We agreed together for this and I followed with a prayer for Rita, asking God to buoy her up in her faith and to cause her to know that God was at work in her family and that he was close to her.

Although our prayers seemed very simple and short, I had nothing more to add, and Greg was silent too. In the few moments of quietness that followed, I felt a little awkward; still no words came, but then I sensed that God was with us in the stillness, and it was OK... it felt right. God was there and that was all that really mattered.

As we continued moving through the crowd there were many people standing with or waiting for an interpreter. There were also some who remained seated and watchful. Each person we prayed for was remarkably different. Some wanted to be healed, several wanted to know more about this, 'Jesus,' while others requested specific prayer for their family. At one point, in between praying, we were approached by a male translator, and Greg was asked for help; an elderly Nepalese man had specifically requested a man to pray for him.

A TIME TO PRAY

As Greg was gone, I stood alone and waited, but only for a moment. Marcel, looking for a prayer partner, approached me and we teamed up. Marcel, a jovial man, tall with broad shoulders and a slightly protruding paunch, talked in a booming voice. His large stature and thick set features made him seem a little intimidating at first, but, after a short space of time, I found Marcel to be the gentle giant who showed a lot of empathy towards others. Although, he did occasionally reveal his serious side, the thing I loved most about Marcel, was that he somehow managed to see the funny side of everything; he nearly always began a conversation with a joke and a laugh.

Marcel and I prayed, in turn, for many complaints of minor ailments such as headaches, sore eyes, skin irritations and stomach upsets as well as other more serious complaints of chronic back pain and joint pain. After I prayed, the Nepali people nearly always said that the pain was reduced or that they, 'felt better.' This was very encouraging at first but then, when I didn't see any improvement, I began to feel a little frustrated. On one occasion, when this happed with a lady whose eyes remained red and watery, I repeated the prayer.

Even after praying a second and third time, despite the woman insisting that her eyes felt much better, I could see that they were no different. I had a sneaking suspicion that the Nepalese people were just being polite and agreeable; it was as though they didn't want to hurt our feelings. I never imagined that there would be a downside to being polite. But these people were such an, 'others focused' people, that they didn't want to embarrass or offend anyone at any cost. Instead they almost always insisted that they were 'feeling better.' I wasn't sure how to deal with the fact that they didn't want to admit it when nothing had changed.

A TIME TO WORK

Many times, this situation repeated itself and it became very dissatisfying to me. All I could do was to draw comfort in knowing that we were totally dependent on the Holy Spirit and on Jesus's name for any healing to take place. With that consolation in mind, I put my frustrations aside and carried on throughout the rest of the day, observing very closely for solid evidence-based, genuine healings.

A TIME TO PLAY

Chapter Eleven

JUNGLE SAFARI

Chitwan National Park, 19th October 2023

*L*ike clockwork I woke up at 3.30am, only today was a free day! There was no teaching session; nothing was planned until much later that morning but it was impossible to go back to sleep. I was glad of the distraction of the upcoming Jungle Safari; the whole team were booked into the 'Chitwan National Park' (CNP). My mind wondered if we might see a Bengal tiger or an elephant, or even a rhino? Greg and I had watched a documentary about CNP, but it had portrayed a bleak story of fewer and fewer sightings of animals in recent years. In the pursuing five hours of waiting, I decided to do a little research of my own, through my friend Wikipedia, to find out a little more.

I found that Chitwan used to be quite a dense forest with many wild animals which attracted big game hunters. It was once known as 'the heart of the jungle' and it became a famous hunting ground where hunters would set up camp for months at a time. Hundreds of elephants, leopards, rhinoceros' and Bengal tigers were shot for trophies, taxidermy, meat and other animal byproducts. The problem of poaching on top of the massive hunting expeditions led to only ninety-five rhinos' remaining in the country by the 1960's.

In 1973 the CNP, Nepal's first National Park, was established as a refuge to protect the endangered single-horned rhinoceros and the Bengal tiger. Today the number of rhinos has increased to 645 in the whole country. The CNP is also home to wild elephants, antelopes, lizards, small crocodiles, gaur (a type of wild oxen) and pythons. There are also numerous species of birds, fish, butterflies and insects as well as abundant types of different grasses, including the elephant grass. I hadn't realised that there were so many animals and birds in the park, and I began to feel a little more excited about the day ahead. (Gurung, K. K. Singh R., 1996)

As we headed down to the dining room, I could see that Greg had little expectation from the Safari. Many of the team were already lining up in a queue for breakfast but they seemed to be more excited about the food than the Safari. We filled our plates with an amazing selection of Nepali food and some limited English food, then sat down to chat. I began to share what I had read, and others shared their expectations and before long the conversations over the table had us all excited.

Waiting outside were three identical open topped, jeep-like trucks (Mahindra Boleros) ready to roll. The jeeps, shaded by a blue cloth canopy each comfortably seated eight people in the open section at the back. The fully enclosed driver's cabin had two seats and was air conditioned. The team looked well prepared donned with impressive cameras, binoculars and safari hats as they boarded the jeeps. We piled into the jeeps randomly; by then we had all become more like over animated 'Tourists on Safari.' It was a surreal feeling, compared to how different it was just the day before, when we were serving others in a more serious role.

The convoy set off. At first it was a smooth ride, that is until we reached a very unimpressive, timber archway. It had just one word, 'Welcome,' painted on it! That was the entrance into the Chitwan National Park. As we drove through the archway, the road remained relatively flat, but it was dry with loose stones, and, from our position at the tail end of the convoy, it was quite dusty. As we continued on the gravel track with thick green foliage either side of us, it became more and more bumpy, but it didn't bother me because I was so focused on keeping my eyes peeled for anything that moved.

'TEAM NEPAL' BEFORE THE SAFARI BEGAN

In the jeep leading the convoy were the highly animated group of Canadians, nicknamed, 'Team Nepal.' They always seemed to be on a high, but today they were absolutely pumped with excitement, even before we began the

safari. Soon into the drive, we heard frequent outbursts of
yelling and cheering with loud uproars of laughter coming
loud and clear even from a good distance away. We found
this to be quite amusing at first. Our attention was captured
by the beautiful emerald landscape all around us as we
focused on spotting an animal. But when we drove for
several kilometres, not seeing a single creature, we began
to realise that it might be due to the loud noises that 'Team
Nepal' was making.

The group in the jeep at the centre of the convoy must
have read our minds as we heard them politely yelling out
to the others in front, 'Quieten down, you're frightening
off the wildlife.' This didn't seem to have much of an
impact. The wild, 'Team Nepal,' just became even more
excited and rowdier. Then, suddenly, the middle jeep
darted out of the convoy and rapidly accelerated passed
Team Nepal's jeep, leaving a cloud of dust in their wake.
Almost immediately, Team Nepal responded by tearing out
from the middle and speedily doing a daring U-turn to join
the convoy at the rear end. Our jeep ended up in a dust
cloud in the centre, but within seconds, our driver accelerated, swung out from the convoy, and took the lead position at the front. We were out of the dust cloud, but it took
a while for Team Nepal to regain composure. After the
massive switcheroo took place only silence remained in the
dust!

Despite our jeep leading at the head of the pack, ever so
quietly rolling through grasslands, wetlands and subtropical
forest and for over an hour, we still hadn't seen anything at
all. This continued for some time, then, finally, as we drove
alongside the huge Bis Hazari Lake, something moved. It
was a small alligator. There were a few of them along the

water's edge, and there were some interesting birds, but no tigers, not even a rhino.

THE COOL TEAM

At this stage, each of the vehicles separated and the drivers coordinated a place to meet up again. After another uneventful hour or so, our driver spotted something. He slowed the jeep right down until it became stationary, and we were told to keep very quiet. Whatever it was, was camouflaged. I scanned the bushes but only when it moved did I get a glimpse of it. My first sighting of a wild animal and I could barely make out what it was! Then it bolted and it was gone in a flash! I was told that it was a magnificent Sambar stag, but my imagination had to fill in the gaps.

SAMBA DEER

The vehicle remained stationary, but then, just a little further away, something else moved. Suddenly, I could see another group of well camouflaged samba deer. There were three or four, huddled together whilst grazing on some shrubs. Looking through binoculars, I could see clearly, that they were smaller in stature with slender bodies, thin legs and reddish brown coats. Their tails were short and stubby but their ears were unusually large and very flappy. Their big, dark eyes peered at us intently as they calmly chewed away. Instead of antlers, I could only see mere fur-covered studs in their place. They were fascinating. They soon became acutely aware of our presence, looking nervous and twitchy, as if about to take flight!

The only photos I had taken all day, were of the rest of the crew in the jeeps. Some had managed to capture bird photos but the only other sighting was a couple of (saddled) apathetic elephants sauntering past us, with a few two-legged creatures riding on top. In spite of that, it was a great day; the excitement and anticipation of not knowing what we might have seen, made the whole experience worthwhile.

Perhaps, if I were ever to revisit the CNP I would arrive much earlier in the morning and I would travel slowly and quietly, on the back of an elephant, through the tall trees and perhaps, I would see a Bengal tiger, a wild elephant, maybe even a leopard or a sloth.

Chapter Twelve

SECOND REMOTE VILLAGE

20th October 2023

I was surrounded by dense jungle forest in torrential rain, alone and yet not afraid. As I slowly advanced on foot, I could hear birds and the sound of rushing water from the nearby waterfall. It was breathtaking. I needed to stop for a pause to take it all in. It was a mystical, enchanting paradise, that is…until I spotted a huge wild cat, just a few meters ahead. Its magnificently streaked body cautiously and slowly moved closer and closer towards me. Mesmerised by its powerful muscles and the symphony of movement in each smooth, gracious step, I froze, but not with fear, rather it was a feeling of awe. Suddenly, it's piercing eyes met mine and its ferocious jaw opened to expose its sharp fangs as it let out a terrifying roar. The lengthy, snarling roar began to diminish and meld into the sound of my alarm clock and suddenly I was fully awake!

In a speedy reflex I killed the alarm before it disturbed Greg, it was only 3.45am and he was still suffering with Delhi-belly. Relieved, not only to escape the Bengal tiger but also that Greg continued to sleep, I crept out of bed and spontaneously splashed my face. In spite of the short sleep, I felt excited about meeting up with the motley bunch for prayer. Each day, our little group grew in number and in faith. The teaching was enriching and I for one, was not disappointed.

The teaching that morning was mainly about small beginnings, how fruitful the early church had been and how, if we adopted that same model (given by Jesus), we too could be fruitful. We listened, we prayed, and we devoured the word, learning about the model of loving and listening to others, of abandoning ourselves to Jesus and becoming dependent upon Him alone. This special time spent with others in God's presence was incomparably more edifying than any other experience I've had.

I couldn't wait to share with Greg all that transpired during the meeting and was so excited that on my return, he was already up and about. Greg was feeling much better and was obviously on the mend. He was keen to hear all about the meeting. What a good long talk we had that morning, and before we knew it, that little window of time just vanished away. We were so deeply engrossed in our conversation that I even missed the prayer walk with Elizabeth (and a third team member) that morning.

By the time we set off to the village I was ready for anything. Outside awaited our coach with the deafening airhorn. It was already loaded with the usual medical supplies, water filters and other goodies to share. The sun was shining after a heavy downpour of rain the night before, but it was just as hot as ever. We boarded the coach and after a quick head count, we were off. The chatter and laughter among the team combined with the noisy airhorn and other competing sounds distracted us most of the time. We rattled along the winding road unaware of any danger until the wide road became less and less wide. The further up the mountain we travelled, the more frequent were the hairpin bends. Our coach often became dangerously close to the cliff edge. We continued, trying not to look too closely, for a number of kilometres. Then our attention was stolen when the coach slowed down and came to an unexpected standstill.

What now? I wondered, but nobody had an immediate answer. After Randeep had made a few phone calls we were told that there was a landslide just ahead, where a small section of the narrow road had slid down the mountain, making it impossible to cross.

The next announcement from Randeep, as he passed around some bottles of water was, 'We need to turn off the motor of the coach, so get hydrated, stay seated and stay calm until we figure this out.' After only five minutes of no air conditioning, the coach became unbearably stifling hot. Many of us prayed for safety and that nothing would hinder us from getting to the village. Thankfully, Randeep quickly realised that there was no quick fix and he suggested that we could leave the coach if we needed to. But he was quick to advise us to keep a sharp lookout for cars and motorbikes and stay close to the coach.

WAITING INSIDE THE COACH

The outside ambience wasn't much different from that of the coach; the air was still and there was no shade to escape from the burning sun. We all seemed to be well prepared with hats and sunnies and although many of us had our own, the sunblock and mosquito repellent was passed around freely. It was soon announced that the only alternative route was a dirt road and that the coach, due to its size and weight on the soft underground, would not be able to make it. We all prayed for safety, wisdom and for God to make a way for us and we sent text messages via the WhatsApp for further prayer cover.

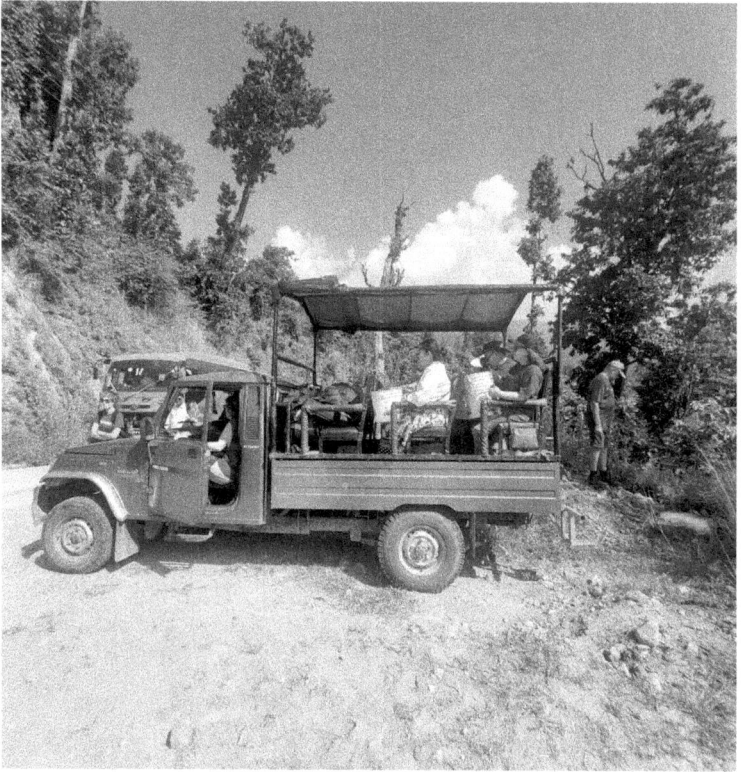

JEEP WITH COACH IN BACKGROUND

Randeep, in coordination with the other leaders, was working on a solution and soon came up with a strategy. The plan was to divide into three groups. One group that could trek the rest of the way to the village, another group that could be transported in three cattle trucks, and a third smaller group, who could go in a Mahindra vehicle with the medical supplies and water filters. Also, a couple of the translators who managed to procure motorcycles (thanks to mobile phones) were able and willing to take pillion passengers.

Everyone began to discuss among themselves which group they would join. Greg and I having had the experience of riding in a cattle truck before, knew which group we wanted to be in. We definitely wanted to walk. The motor cycles arrived and after what seemed like a long wait, the Mahindra also arrived.

In the meantime, we joined the walking group, but just as the group were about to start the trek, Randeep approached me and in a very determined manner, advised me that, 'It's hot, it's uphill and it's very slippery underfoot.' I smiled at him, and responded, 'Greg and I will be trekking in altitude at the end of this trip, so this will be a good training opportunity.'

Randeep just walked away, shaking his head. At that point Greg didn't want me to walk either and he too suggested that I would be better in the truck. Before I could respond, the first cattle truck arrived, and all the medical team were asked to climb aboard. I didn't make a move but Randeep returned and continued to dissuade me from walking.

He insisted that I was needed to help with setting up the clinic. 'But I'm on the prayer team today,' I thought to myself. Although I remained silent, my thoughts raged... 'I'm not even allocated to the clinic.' I was so angry, but I could see that Randeep wasn't happy either. I could see that he thought he had a point. I didn't try to correct him. Still, I hesitated to follow his instructions and stood my ground. Then Greg gave me that look, and walked away without a word. The look that says, 'You know you should.'

Greg picked up his pace to catch up to the rest of the walkers. The cattle truck was waiting but I wavered all the more, at that point, Genevieve's voice became demanding as she hollered out, 'Just get in the truck Bridget.' That made me dig my heels in and hesitate even further, but this time I knew I was just being stubborn. I knew that I should comply.

When Genevieve frantically repeated again, 'Just get in the truck,' I was so reluctant, but I conformed. It wasn't easy to give in to my stubbornness. Even though I slowly moved towards the direction of the truck, I was still thinking (heatedly) of how unfair it was that Greg could walk but I couldn't.

CATTLE TRUCK SETTING OFF

Out of the blue, one of the key points I had been reading from the notes on spiritual preparation, dropped into my psyche. 'Be prepared to lay down your rights.' Unexpectedly, and almost instantly, I felt a little ashamed for being so resistant and selfish, then, I asked myself, 'How could I possibly pray for people, with such an attitude?'

I sadly realised that I was giving the devil a foothold and as soon as I climbed into the truck, I confessed my self-ishness. Immediately after that, I found relief from my anger, it just seemed to dissipate, and from that moment my attitude began to change.

CATTLE TRUCK ARRIVING AT VILLAGE

There was still room for one more person on the truck; this time it was Hector who was being persuaded to join us. In fact, the wheels of the truck had begun to roll as he half-heartedly hopped onto the back step. With one leg in and one leg out, Hector was being violently jerked about as he straddled the tailgate, and as the truck picked up speed he had to cling on for dear life. In spite of it all, the man with the plaits poking out of his visor cap, was still smiling! The harshness of being jolted around was such a challenge for all of us, even though the truck was only moving very slowly.

It was incredibly hot and sticky under the scorching sun and the rough road soon became even rougher. Within a short distance we were on a dirt track and we were travelling up a steep slope, incredibly slowly, so slowly that we could have walked quicker. Every time the wheels hit the potholes our sweaty bodies jarred against each other. That's when I wished I had been allowed to walk. But just when I was wishing it, as if it were a sign, we passed the walkers and I could see that they were making extremely slow progress as they tackled the gruelling climb over muddy, ankle twisting terrain; I soon changed my mind and stopped wishing. In a feeble attempt to encourage the men as we passed, some shouted out ... 'Champions ... Our heroes' and other positive words.

Only a couple of kilometres up the dirt track the truck slipped sideways in the mud and plunged into a very deep pothole. There were a few sharp intakes of breath, and some groans. My knuckles turned white as I clung with a death grip onto the bars, while others let out shrieks of terror as their bodies pressed hard against one another. Inevitably, the front wheel just kept spinning unable to gain traction; we were bogged in. We all piled off to lighten the load, and ironically, we ended up walking in the mud for a small section of the way, after all. The second cattle truck caught up and while they passed us, they openly cheering us on.

Eventually, with a little persuasion, our truck managed to free itself and we all piled back into it. The truck was struggling with the weight, so, when we got closer to the village, we were offered the opportunity to walk the rest of the way. I eagerly accepted it with relief; I couldn't get off that truck quickly enough!

NATURAL BUBBLE PLANT

We were led through the bush on a firm grassy surface by one of the Nepalese locals; it was a shortcut to the village and a very pleasant one too. The air felt fresh as we walked through a thick verdant canopy of trees and bush. Along the way, one of the Nepalese Doctors stopped and pulled off a few leaves from a particular shrub; he then snapped the stalk and began to blow on it. Immediately numerous bubbles floated up into the air; it was a natural bubble plant. Fascinated, I copied his actions but I soon discovered that it was quite an art. I couldn't produce a single bubble. The doctor chuckled at my failures and then he instructed me on how to do it. Once I got the hang of it, it worked like magic. The trick was, to break the stalk at the right place, and to blow ever so gently. Ironically, we foreigners had brought bubbles which ran out within minutes and the locals already had their own bubble plant which never ran out! Amazing!

The whole experience certainly turned out to be a great team building exercise which extended across cultures to our Nepalese friends and translators. It also got the adrenalin flowing, which made us determined to bring Christ to the people we served, and it kept us going all throughout the day.

The clinic had already been set up by the group who had arrived long before us on the jeep. We were all ready to roll but the walkers had still not yet arrived! I was a little concerned and enquired after them, and to my great relief, I was told that the first truck had gone back to pick them up. I waited eagerly for Greg and the walkers to arrive, and they did eventually arrive, looking like they had just stepped out of a sauna. They too had been dropped off and had walked the last leg by way of the shortcut.

THE WALKERS - SHORT CUT

After a short while greeting the walkers, we were each directed to our allocated groups. I set off to the area already set-up for prayer and looked around for Basanta. He arrived as cheerful as ever and we had a little window of time to catch up before our first patient. I asked Basanta about his faith. I was curious to know as to what motivated him, a Hindu, to be a translator for a Christian organisation. 'So, what do **you** believe in Basanta,' I asked in a curious manner. Basanta, very openly said, 'I'm Hindu, but I don't practice my beliefs as much as I should.' He confessed.

'How come,' I responded.

'I'm too busy,' he said, quickly followed by, 'with study and work and volunteering here.'

'Tell me then, what religious things would you be doing if you had time?' I asked.

Basanta looked at me intently, responding with a smile and said, 'Maybe I'd spend more time in the temple praying.'

'Who do you pray to, Basanta,' I enquired.

'Our family doesn't favour any particular god,' he explained. 'We have many gods, so it could be any one of them.'

'It must be hard to get to know all of them,' I exclaimed.

'There are too many, I don't really worry about that,' he said, 'I just try to be a good person because I believe in Karma,'. At that point, I could see a lady, who was slightly bent over, hobbling towards us and I quickly ended our conversation, saying, 'I'd like to know more about Karma, can we continue this conversation another time?' Basanta looked relieved and he agreed happily.

The middle-aged lady approached looking worn out and anxious, her name is Alina. She began talking about her back pain before she even sat down. I wanted to closely observe the amount of mobility before and after I prayed, so I stepped a few paces away and asked her to walk as straight as she could towards me. Her brow creased and she grimaced as if the pain prevented her from fully straightening up. I watched her very carefully. With every other step she placed her hand on her back and flinched. I then ushered her to sit down and sat beside her. Basanta sat on the other side and began translating. We went through the usual questions and Alina described how the pain slowed her down and how it limited the distance she could go without pain relief. She had had the pain for many years. It sounded like and looked like a case of advanced scoliosis.

I was overcome with compassion towards Alina, she was so hopeful and she had made such a big effort to get to the clinic. When it came time to pray specifically for healing, I spoke quietly and told Jesus that I believed he could move mountains. Then I placed my hand, with Alina's permission, on the area causing the pain and fully believing for a complete healing. With a stronger authoritative voice, I said, 'I commanded this back pain to go in the name of Jesus,' and continued, 'In the name of Jesus, spinal cord receive healing.' I then paused and asked Alina how she felt. Her forehead wrinkled as she raised her eyebrows in a surprized look, she stood up, just a little straighter, and stated with amazement, 'It's gone, the pain has gone!'

Alina seemed different, more relaxed even happy, so I asked her if she could stand up. She did so immediately, then I asked if she could walk just a few meters. Alina nodded and began to walk away from me. At first, she took a few sheepish steps, but with each step her back straightened a little more and I could see definite improvement, she picked up her pace and just kept going. I realised that she wasn't going to stop, so I yelled out after her by name but she couldn't hear me. I laughed and covered my mouth with one hand in amazement. It was such a happy but surreal moment. Alina was now such a good distance away that Basanta had to run after her. Together they walked back side by side at a normal pace, both with beaming smiles all over their faces. Alina was so thankful. I made sure that she knew it was Jesus that had healed her, and I asked her if we could thank Him. She nodded in joyful agreement and we prayed together. Alina walked away that day with a spring in her step, a much different person. This euphoric experience caused my expectations to soar. I was so reassured and felt stronger in my faith. This was a genuine healing, a healing that I had witnessed with my own eyes.

The very next person I prayed for was a lady called Gopini. Gopini had stomach pain with a sensation of burning. I laid my hand on her stomach (once given permission) and prayed in a similar way as before. After I'd finished, in a very polite way, Gopini said that she felt much better. It wasn't anything that I could see or test but I simply accepted it as a true healing. Just before finishing up, I noticed Gopini's right hand. It was small and emaciated and was held tightly clenched in a fist. On further enquiry she explained that she was born with a shrivelled hand and that she was used to it. The main hindrance was that she couldn't find employment because of it. I asked her if I could pray for her hand to be restored. Gopini looked at me a little surprised but she nodded in a positive but nonchalant way. I cradled her withered hand in my hands and held it securely while I paused to listen to God. After a short silence, I felt absolutely sure that God was saying He wanted to heal Gopini's hand. It was more of an impression than an audible voice with words. I prayed with a sense of authority but in a quiet, fervent way, 'Thank you God that you love Gopini and that you are more than able to restore her hand. In the name of Jesus, I command this hand to stretch out and be healed.' I opened my hands in full expectation of seeing Gopini's hand begin to stretch out. Nothing appeared to be happening and after a moment, I asked Gopini, 'Does your hand feel any different?' Without any words, she responded by shaking her head.

Still hopeful, I turned to Basanta and asked him to confirm with Gopini if we could keep praying. My eyes returned to Gopini as she nodded. Without saying anything, I continued looking straight into Gopini's eyes, and with confidence I stated, 'Gopini, God wants to heal your hand.'

She simply nodded and I prayed again, but again nothing happened. Hope began to ebb away, nevertheless, in desperation I repeated the prayer one more time. Yet still, no visible change. Gopini's hand was not healed. I was devastated. I couldn't understand why the miracle I believed for didn't happen.

Surprisingly to me, Gopini didn't appear to mind, she just kept expressing how happy she was that her stomach was no longer burning. I felt that I too should be grateful, but my mind went into overdrive with questions trying to work it all out. I just couldn't fathom why I had felt so certain of a complete healing. I was so sure… and yet so wrong.

Knowing that God wants to heal people and knowing that He is fully able to do so, this experience just did not compute. I was uncomfortable and wanted to retreat with the many questions that needed to be answered, but there were people waiting and I had to move on. I continued with much less confidence in what I was doing and saying. All throughout the rest of the morning, there were ups and downs. Some people were healed, some simply 'felt better,' and some were not healed at all. I was left unable to figure out anything. There was no rhyme or reason and I became more uncertain about healing than I had started out with. When lunch was announced, I breathed a sigh of relief.

LUNCH IS SERVED

A giant pot of rice and another extremely large pot of the most amazing curry was prepared by our familiar Chef and was served by several of the team. The rest of us enjoyed mingling and eating with the locals wherever there was a space to sit on the grass. Although the language barrier made it difficult to talk directly with the Nepali people, it was made possible through a few willing translators. After several conversations, I noted that some of the Nepalese people, particularly the young men, were returning for seconds. That's when I took the opportunity to catch up with the rest of the prayer team and hear about their experiences. The conversations were very positive and were focused on the miracles that had taken place, not the ones that hadn't.

Lunch was finally winding down when everyone was satiated. I was drawn to the music of the strings playing in the background and the sound lifted my spirits. Samuel began to strum his guitar and Prathna, his sister, began to sing in her usual spirited manner. She sang in English at first and then switched to an Indian dialect with a song which had an energy all of its own. The team joined in enthusiastically clapping, followed by a few Nepalese women who began to sing along while swaying and clapping. As the clapping became louder and louder, more women, some children, and a few of the men were drawn into the joyful atmosphere of worship. Heaven invaded the ground we stood on and it made me glad.

CROSS-CULTURAL WORSHIP

THE WORSHIP TEAM

As we all worshipped melodiously together, I saw the youthful and energetic Prathna, so young yet so aware of God, with her amazing ability to worship openly and freely and I wished I was young again. This beautiful young woman with long, straight black hair and clear olive skin inspired me; she appeared to be sincerely and passionately enjoying every moment of the worship. I found myself pondering over the question, 'What would it be like to have known Jesus in my youth?' And I reflected on how different my life could have been.

I felt that Prathna was so blessed and I realised that we are the way we are, because of our upbringing and the events which we are exposed to. But then I grasped the reality of where I had come from, and the fact that Jesus somehow had reached down and pulled me out of the fire and I knew, that I too was blessed beyond comprehension. Right then, misty eyed, I thanked God for loving me.

After much singing, Randeep began his sermon, again in a dialect that the people understood. We gathered around, mostly standing; the team randomly mixed in with the crowd of Nepalese people. They were listening, while we were silently praying for their souls to be saved and their lives restored. The atmosphere was changing and again the impression that something deeply spiritual was happening continued. People all through the crowd began to put up their hands and Randeep gave instructions in English for to us to find a translator and approach anyone whose hand was raised and to pray with them.

The message of the Gospel had been preached and the whole team, including the translators, were ready and available to pray for those who had responded. Often, the prayer requests were for prayer for other member of the family who couldn't attend. This was due to, either chronic pain or immobility from untreated injuries. Sometimes, it was for their family who didn't approve of them becoming a Christian. Others wanted to give their lives to Jesus. For whatever the reason, praying for these spiritually sensitive people and seeing its effect was undeniably miraculous.

The return trip was uneventful, it was dark outside and most of us were just tired, even too tired to talk. In this fairly quiet and safe space on the coach, I found myself reflecting on the experience with Gopini over and over, but with no resolve. Finally, I gave it to God and asked Him to show me what He wanted to teach me through this experience and then I waited for an answer!

Chapter Thirteen

DEBRIEF

he answer came through a debriefing session on that same day. In our care group, I wanted to bring up the subject of authenticity and the conflict that I was feeling about some of the claims to healing by the Nepalese people.

Our team leader, a senior woman, Deb Runstedler, was a curiously delightful, old-fashioned lady from Canada. Her simple hair style of greying waves drooping down around her ageing face seemed to mask the fact that she was a very interesting person. I discovered that Deb had travelled the world and experienced more than most other people of her generation; she was full of surprises. Every wrinkle told a story of her life and struggles, she was a remarkably open and honest person who engaged very easily in conversation.

Deb began our debriefing session with a prayer and then she threw out a question, 'How are you all feeling today?' she said in a quiet and thoughtful way. A pregnant silence followed as Deb looked form one person to the other, but there was no response. I was feeling disappointed and my thoughts were consumed with Gopini and others who had not been healed, when Deb's eyes landed on me. I hesitated, but felt compelled to respond. I couldn't think of any other words to describe how I felt, so I just said, 'Disappointed!'

'Why, what happened?' Deb replied in a surprised way. In my frustration I just let loose and expressed how I was feeling. 'The prayer experience has been like a rollercoaster for me', I stated. 'I don't understand why God heals one person, but not the other. And, the Nepalese people are so polite, they almost never say anything negative or contrary to the expectation of healing. Most of the time they just agree that they feel better even though it's obvious that nothing has changed. It's so frustrating!' I exclaimed.

I described the woman (Alina) who was truly healed and how obvious it was by her ability to walk and by the excitement and joy expressed on her face. I explained that I knew her healing was without question, authentic, and how the experience had boosted my faith to such a degree that it seemed like nothing was impossible for God.

Then I shared how Gopini came along and how she had received instant relief from the burning in her stomach. I explained about Gopini's hand and how I was so sure that it would be healed. So sure, that I had even spoken it out to her. But after praying, nothing happened, even after praying three times … nothing! I became a little emotional as I stated, 'I really believed but it didn't happen'. After a caring pause, Deb responded softly, 'It may still happen.' She continued, 'We don't always see the complete healing, but that doesn't mean it hasn't begun.'

Interrupting the silence that followed, Hector, revealing

his serious side asked, 'How did that experience affect your prayer for others afterwards?'

'I just continued to pray,' I said. 'But I felt that I was on shaky ground.'.

'The important thing is that you continued to believe and you continued to pray,' Hector responded.

The whole group engaged in deep conversation for some time. I want to share just a few of the many thoughts that we agreed upon, one being, that our confidence should not and cannot be in ourselves because it's not about us, or what we are doing, it's about God and what He is doing. It's only when our confidence is in God, that we can persist in prayer.

Another thought was that when we question God with questions like, 'What did I do wrong? Why was the person not healed?' These questions only lead to the feeling of failure. Our failure is unfounded, as it's not us that's doing the healing in the first place. It's God's job to heal, so how can we fail? Does this mean that God has failed? No, of course not. We know that God is more than able to heal any affliction. If we trust God, and if we are confident that God is faithful, and know without doubt that He is our sovereign God, then why do we feel disappointed? In this particular case the answer did not come easy.

I concluded that I had not fully surrendered my will to God's will. It was me who wanted the healing not Gopini. Accepting God's sovereign will without question is an ongoing struggle for me, but I acknowledge my struggle and I carry on trusting in His faithfulness and mercy towards me.

After the debrief, I realised that I could never assume 'to know' what God was going to do.

For we are God's masterpiece, created in Christ Jesus to
do good works, which God prepared in advance for us.
                                                    (Ephesians 2:10)

Why God did not heal Gopini remains a mystery to me, but how can I, the created, possibly question the ultimate creator of all things. *God knows what He is doing.* I needed to let go of asking 'why' and to cease trying to work it out. It was beyond my understanding. I made a conscious decision from then on to persist in confident prayer for healing and to acknowledge that God always has the final say. This empowered me to continue praying for people regardless of the outcome, and to accept God's will over mine. I was encouraged to realise that we can never fully understand His ways, but that we can unequivocally persist in pursuing the mystery of Christ!

On the other side of the coin, when a genuine healing did take place, I was in awe and always felt astounded and so very grateful for the privilege of being a conduit for that healing and for being an eyewitness!

Debrief continued with Iana sharing, in her gentle Canadian accent, about the initial difficulty she had experienced on arrival to Nepal when her foot became very swollen. At first, she had thought it was simply the result of the long hall flight from Ontario. A day later after resting and having her leg elevated the swelling worsened, so much so that even the slightest movement made Iana wince as she shifted position. She also developed a fever and became quite sick.

One of the doctors was called to examine Iana and discovered a tiny perforation in the reddened area of her foot; the doctor prescribed antibiotics as she thought it was possibly due to a spider bite which had developed into cellulitis. The pain and discomfort very much limited Iana's mobility and she couldn't join in most of the activities during those initial few days.

Iana articulated well about how upset and disheartened she had felt in the first couple of days, but also how she had sensed God's presence comforting her and providing all that she needed during that time. Iana was so grateful for the (team) doctors who attended her, for the other team members around her and for the fact that God had made a way for her to participate in the first medical clinic day.

Marcel, the gentle giant, and his wife Iana, like Greg and I, were on our first ever Journey of Compassion, so everything was new to us, and we were all part of the same care group. Marcel did everything he could to make Iana comfortable during that difficult time, he was clearly devoted to Iana.

During that debriefing, Marcel was so excited and keen to share about what he had seen. He spoke in awe of the miracles that he had witnessed, he never mentioned anyone that wasn't healed, nor did he mention any concerns about anything at all. Being the caring character that he was, Marcel was probably aware of allowing time for the rest of the group to share.

The fifth member of our care group was the cool, easy-going Hector with his chilled Caribbean accent. His role in the pharmacy kept him busy and meant that he was mostly unable to get around and witness anything outside of the pharmacy during the mornings. Hector was therefore in listening mode rather than sharing mode but he was able to contribute some positive and valuable ideas into all our conversations.

Although Joan, the prayer team leader, wasn't in any particular care group, she dropped in and out of all the groups at some stage or another. Joan, a short, solid woman with shoulder length salt and pepper hair, which she always tucked behind her ears, introduced herself in a positive and confident manner.

That day, it was our pleasure to have this little woman drop in on our group to pray with/for us. Her height hardly reflected her big heart in tune with God and the encouragement that she was to all of us. Joan really added value to the debriefing session by helping us to work through some of the difficult questions.

Not that she came up with all the answers, but we did reach a point of understanding that *we don't need to know everything,* and of accepting that God is in control. This may not seem revolutionary to some, but to me it reaffirmed my need to let go and let God. In turn this led to allowing myself to be stretched and changed daily.

Going back to the debriefing session after our first visit to a remote village, I realised that even though we were all on the same Journey of Compassion at the same village, everyone's experience was uniquely different. My time working in the mobile clinic was so totally different to that of Greg's encounter with the water filter team.

While I worked inside most of the day, Greg and his group worked outside. They walked around the village, in and out of people's homes, bringing water filters. Their role was to install the filters, as well as to instruct both men and women on how to use and maintain them in good working order. By meeting people in their own homes and talking with families, they actually had an amazing opportunity to see first-hand what village life looked like.

WATER FILTERS ARE DISTRIBUTED

On another occasion, while I was on the prayer team in the second village, Greg had the opportunity to share something close and personal of himself, of how he came to know Jesus at a deeper level. He shared with a mixed group of mainly men, and a few women. The point Greg made was that for many, many years he knew about Jesus, but that it was simply 'head knowledge,' an intellectual exercise which he could pick up and put down whenever he chose. The head knowledge wasn't enough by itself, he explained. It had to pass to, 'heart knowledge,' before he could truly embrace faith in Jesus. It was only when he believed, with his heart, that his life 'dramatically changed forever.'

SHARING A PERSONAL TESTIMONY

All through the day each of the clinics were filled with so much activity, both inside the little hall and outside under the sun. Homes were visited, testimonies shared, the gospel was preached, water filters installed, children entertained and amused with all sorts of drawing materials, games and bubbles, and many of the Nepalese women participated in the times of praise and worship with singing and dancing. Most importantly, prayer was lavished on all who wanted it, and there were many.

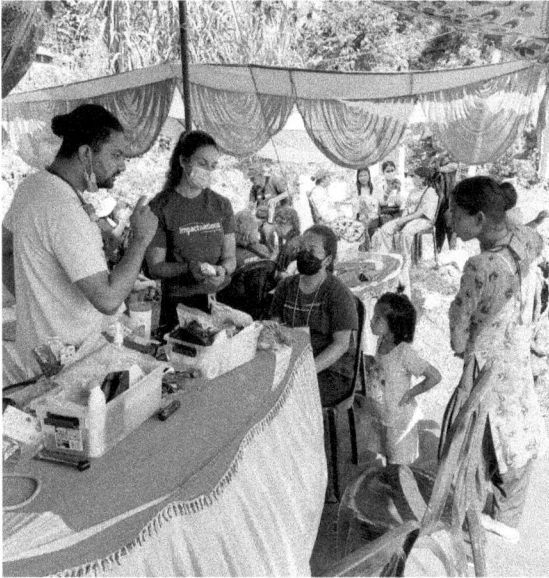

MEDICAL CLINIC IN ACTION

What an awesome privilege, that God allows us mere mortals to participate with Him by being living testimonies of His goodness. Even more astounding is that He blessed us even further by adding new souls to His Kingdom and by heeling people before our very eyes during a JOC!

Chapter Fourteen

NEPALI CHURCH

21st October 2023

We were all invited to attend two different churches and to accept both invitations, we split into two smaller groups. Our group attended the remote village where we had set up our first Medical Clinic three days earlier; that same little multipurpose hall was used for many things including church on Saturdays. As we approached the yellow building, with steps leading up to the hall, we could hear singing and loud clattering of musical instruments. The service was well attended by those who lived close by as well as by those who had walked for some distance on foot from the neighbouring villages. Others had travelled even longer distances, riding motorbikes loaded with pillion passengers, usually the whole family; wife (sitting side-saddle in a sari) and one or two children squashed in-between, even though the law in Nepal says that, *'A motorcycle must not carry more than one pillion rider and he/she must sit astride the machine on a proper seat and should keep both feet on the footrests.'* I guess the nature of remote areas makes the law impossible for police to keep.

It was quite surprising, walking into the hall. Everyone was sitting on the timber floor, even the elderly, grey-haired women sat cross legged on the floor. A wide aisle was created down the centre of the hall, created by the division of women and children sitting on one side, segregated from the men on the opposite side. To my relief, we were guided to the back of the hall, where a single row of plastic seats had been set-up especially for us.

Almost immediately after we entered the church, the singing began to peter out to nothing as the Nepalese pastor (through a translator) began to speak. After a few warm words of welcome, he explained that the congregation would like to welcome us in their own cultural way. The pastor then reverted to Nepalese and addressed the congregation who became strangely quiet. The clinic had become God's house from my perspective, though, I guess from their perspective it was the other way around.

The atmosphere in the hall was starkly different from that of the hustle and bustle of the clinic just a few days before; although it was chock-a-block with people, there was complete and utter silence. It was so quiet. I swear I could have heard my heartbeat. A deep sense of reverence and respect filled the air, even the children were captivated by the silence.

Each of us visitors were welcomed in the traditional way with a white sash or Khata. This simple rectangular cloth represents honour and respect and is a deeply spiritual symbol of protection, connection and empowerment. The sash was placed around our neck by the women folk, one by one, and a special blessing was prayed over each of us individually. Once we had all received a blessing, the congregation began to clap their hands fervently. The clapping went on for an extended period. I was surprised at just how long it went on, and I was touched to the core, as I'm sure were the others.

When the clapping finally stopped, a small group of young Nepali people sang songs of worship. They also played music using the most unusual instruments; there was a handheld drum, as well as different wind and string instruments. The whole congregation joined in heartily singing. Although I couldn't understand a word, some of the songs were recognisable as they had the same melody as our songs. We could virtually join in by singing the words in our language and still harmonise with them singing in theirs. The sound of voices and the sense of hearts yearning for God, along with the pounding of instruments in praise of the Savior, was extraordinary. These believers were singing from the heart and in their own cultural context. For me it was a splendid encounter; a tiny taste of that glorious day! I reflected on how Christianity was so relevant even in their culture, in many other diverse cultures too. It's not just a mere import from Colonialism'. I looked around the hall as I sang joyfully and a verse from the book of Revelations became very real to me...

'*After this I looked, and there before me was a great multitude that no one could count, from every nation, tribe, people and language, standing before the throne and before the Lamb.*'

(*Revelation 7:9a*)

GATHERING AFTER CHURCH

The pastor continued the service speaking in his native language, he spoke for a very long time. With no creche available and no toys to play with I was amazed at how well behaved the children were; even the toddlers were able to sit still and quiet for extended periods.

We had been given an invitation to share about our faith walk or a scripture, during the service, Marcel and Greg had accepted the invite. They were informed that communion would take place halfway into the sermon and that the pastor would call them up to speak sometime during his sermon. I think, having communion in the middle of the sermon, made it seem longer. For communion, the men lined up first and the women and children followed. After communion, when it seemed well into the sermon, Marcel and Greg were on tenterhooks expecting to be called up at any given moment. The pastor's sermon, however, went on for eons!

At last, Marcel was ushered to the front to speak, he was so much taller and broader than the Nepalese men and he could project his booming voice very well. Although given a microphone, Marcel hardly needed it.

He preached from Genesis 37 about the story of Joseph's life, describing how Joseph had been given dreams by God to show that he would, one day, rule over his brothers. Joseph's brothers became jealous and attacked him and sold him into slavery. What followed was the most difficult trials in Joseph's life but in spite of his many years of suffering, he never gave up on God, he never doubted the dreams, he simply believed that God had a plan for his life.

And of course, the dreams eventually came to pass and Joseph saved his brothers and his people from starving during the famine. Marcel brought a message of hope and encouragement which I felt was most appropriate, considering the tough times the Nepalese people seemed to go through.

When the worship group began to sing again, I thought the service would never end. I doubted (and hoped) that there wouldn't be enough time for Greg to speak and in fact, there wasn't. I was relieved, as I'm sure all of us were, when at the end of the singing, the service finally concluded. Greg was still feeling tired from the previous day's clinic and he seemed pleased but at the same time, just a fraction disappointed.

After church we returned to the hotel for lunch which was followed by a debriefing session. Firstly, we spent some time in the safe place of our small care groups, and shared experiences good and bad. We nearly always had questions but hardly ever had any grievances.

The collection of team shirts for washing, explanation of the following day's plans and an opportunity for questions ended our debriefing session.

VILLAGE PRAYER WALK

That Saturday afternoon was scheduled for some free

time, but we were also given an alternative option of participating in a prayer walk in one of the villages with pastor Randeep. Greg and I jumped at the opportunity...this is what we came for! I wanted, more than anything to be active in my prayer life and to bring God's kingdom down to earth and see His healing and transformative power at work. Like most of the team (except for the few who were still unwell) we all gladly chose to go on the prayer walk.

The sun was shining and the sky was blue when we set off on the coach to the village, but not long after alighting from the bus, some dark ominous clouds began to form. There were only a scarce few local people outside, it was very quiet. We decided to split-up into two smaller groups and began to walk in opposite directions, hoping that a smaller group might be more approachable.

Still, we didn't get any invites into the homes. However, within a short time, it began to rain, but the rain was only light so we continued walking in the rain. I noted that the ground quickly became muddy as the mud stuck firmly to my hiking boots and was building up at an alarming rate. Just as the rain began to pour down, an elderly woman appeared on her front porch and ushered us into her home.

We all huddled under the small entrance porch where most of us could stand out of the rain. The lady humbly requested that we remove our muddy boots and shoes; she then invited us in. The house was only tiny and even though we had split into smaller groups, we were still many, so not all of us could fit inside. A few of us chose to remain at the front door under the porch; we stood around the open doorway looking in. Though I couldn't see much through everyone gathered inside, I could hear almost everything that was said.

INSIDE A VILLAGE HOME

The translator was introduced to the woman's husband who politely asked if we could pray for his son. He explained that his son had been unable to walk to the clinic. The spokesperson for our group was led to an adult man who lay propped up in bed in the corner of the room. He explained that he had been bedridden for the past week with severe pain from an old injury to his leg and he wanted to be healed. This invitation gave me great faith to believe for a miracle, it was as though God had orchestrated the rain on our behalf. God calls us to be co-workers with Him and He allows us to stand in the gap for others. So, there we were, like excited little children, hoping, trusting and believing that God would move His mighty hand, simply because we were seeking His will, we were asking in prayer and we were collectively believing that He would hear us.

Keep on asking, and you will receive what you ask for. Keep on seeking, and you will find. Keep on knocking, and the door will be opened to you.

(Matthew 7:7).

As the young man spoke, his story unfolded until, when he attempted to move his leg, he groaned with pain and his face became distorted. On resting his leg, he described how he had been using a digging tool, similar to a mattock, when he accidently sliced into his leg right down to the shin bone. This had happened some years ago, but he had never seen a doctor and although the wound had healed, he continued to suffer unpredictable bouts of severe pain from the old wound. The young man had been able to walk, in between these painful episodes, but he had not been able to return to work as before.

After hearing his story, the person nearby the young man laid his hands on the man's shin and began to pray out loud. He called on the authority of Jesus Christ and commanded the pain to go and the leg to be restored to total health. While he was praying, I began to pray quietly in my heart and in tongues. I could hear the occasional voice from others indicating that they were in agreement with the prayer. After praying, the young man was asked if he felt any relief or change. 'Just a little,' he responded. The next request was to see if he could move his leg. When he attempted to do so, his facial expression clearly showed that the movement caused a fair amount of pain.

A second prayer was suggested and the man agreed. Afterwards, although the man said again, that he felt, 'Slightly better,'… he grimaced with pain on movement. We all had a burning desire to see him healed and a third prayer was said over him. This time the man said that the pain was reduced and he wanted to attempt to stand up. He managed to weight bear and stand on his leg for a moment, then he took a step, but within a few seconds it was obvious that he was in pain. The young man was guided back into his bed and encouraged to believe that the healing had begun and that it would continue over the coming days or weeks.

I couldn't help but feel a little disappointed. Despite my disappointment, I knew not to ask the 'Why' question, instead I simply acknowledged that God was in control, that His ways are higher than our ways and that He deeply cares for this man. It was only then that I was able to let go of my will and accept God's sovereign will. Although acceptance of the outcome didn't come easy, when I embraced it, an unexpected sense of peace filled my heart, and it was well with my soul.

We continued on the prayer walk and found that there were some people in the village who had already accepted Jesus, they simply wanted to be encouraged in their faith. Praying for their family members by name encouraged them not to give up but to continue praying and to keep on believing for them.

The rain continued, it was a much heavier downpour and we were getting soaked. We decided to head for shelter and waited to see if it might clear. It didn't, and there wasn't a soul in sight, so at that point we realised that our opportunity to pray for others had come to an end and we called it a day.

Chapter Fifteen

THIRD REMOTE VILLAGE

22nd October 2023

*M*y day began with the early teaching session, but instead of the joining the prayer walk afterwards, with Elizabeth, I spent some time with Greg. Following breakfast, we were all gathered in the conference room for morning worship. Adam was speaking when suddenly, mid-sentence, he was interrupted by Bill bursting into the room in quite an unsettling way, urgently exclaiming, 'We must evacuate the building immediately.' Bill continued in a raised voice, 'Do not go to your room for anything … leave now!' He then immediately ushered us out the door and as we left the room he repeatedly said, 'Regroup outside in the car park now!' We had no idea what was going on. I had even thought it might have been a fire drill but quickly dismissed that notion because of Bill's intensity and his disturbing tone. During orientation, we were told that if we ever heard the words, 'leave now,' we were to do it without question and take it very seriously.

Once outside, we regrouped and found that staff and patrons alike had already gathered there; none of the team really knew what was going on until we enquired of others. Apparently, there had been an earthquake relatively close to the hotel and there were concerns of a second earthquake or aftershocks to follow. Not knowing what to expect, we prayed for safety, and after a short time of waiting with no further news, we alerted our various prayer partners on WhatsApp about the situation. I was comforted at that time, to know that people across the globe were praying with us.

After waiting patiently outside for approximately half an hour, nothing had changed. No further reports of after-shock had been reported, and the staff began to return to their posts. Bill, in a much calmer manner, approached and informed us to meet back in the conference room.

He was composed when he addressed the whole group, but by his tone, he was clearly not happy. He reprimanded us for not listening to him or following his instructions. Apparently, some team members had returned to their rooms to retrieve items instead of heading straight outside. Bill explained that although we were fortunate this time, there could have been imminent danger and he made it clear that we must follow his instructions, especially when he uses the words, 'Leave now'. The message came across loud and clear to everyone in the team!

Apparently, the earthquake of magnitude: 5.3 on the Richter Scale had jolted Nepal, striking Kathmandu, and the shock waves had reached as far as Chitwan. However, no report of any death or damage resulted from the tremor.

The three separate jeeps awaited us, and we were at last on our way to our final clinic. Very little rain had fallen since the last big downpour and our drive was uneventful. In thirty-seven-degree heat, the colourful crowd of villagers stood waiting under the blazing sun, and still they greeted us with open arms. Despite the warm 'Namaste' welcomes and the smiles on their faces, the tell-tale beads of sweat on their foreheads made them look how I felt; very hot and sweaty. The only shaded section, in this relatively flat open area, was a tiny patch of grass beneath a thin red and yellow canopy made of cloth.

Randeep announced that before we commenced the clinic, the village community wanted to honour us with a presentation of some wreaths. The villagers had made the wreaths by hand out of some wildflowers growing in the local area. We were all ushered to form a line in between the tables under the shade of the canopy but there was barely enough space to accommodate all of us, so we huddled together.

After some kind words of appreciation from one spokeswoman, (through a translator) we were each individually approached by two ladies. One lady carried a large bunch of wreaths and the other presented us with a separate wreath. It was a unique experience for me. With the utmost respect, one of the ladies put a wreath around my neck, in a very natural and dignified way, she formed praying hands, closed her eyes and bowed her head down slowly without saying a word. My heart was touched in a deep way; it was unlike anything I'd experienced before. A long pause followed, during which time, a strong sense of deeply connected spirituality invaded that space. The warmth and the peaceful feeling I felt is impossible to describe fully. As the woman slowly opened her eyes and made contact with mine, her modest smile turned into a radiant beaming smile of approval. I'm sure that she had also encountered that same warmth and that she had perceived that same transcendent aspect of deep connection with God which I had felt. All I could do, was to reflect her smile in a joyous moment of unity. The woman continued towards Greg, who was standing right next to me. When he received his wreath, I could see that he was touched by the sentiment in a similarly deep way.

WREATHS OF GRATITUDE

After all the various challenges of the morning it was so refreshing to know that the Nepalese people were truly appreciative of the team's effort. By the time everyone received their wreath, we felt ready to pour ourselves out in full expectation of seeing God move in and through us. With the whole day ahead of us, we eagerly got to work setting up the tables that had been put out for us.

In the small, shaded area, on four large tables, the clinic team equipment was set-up. To the front of the open grassy patch was a tiny pink and grey brick building with rows of plastic green chairs placed in the sun alongside it. One large table with a green and yellow tablecloth was set aside for serving the main meal. That too was in the sun since there was no space left under the canopy. I was allocated to helping in the pharmacy that day.

My role was to explain and clarify the dosage and frequency of the medications prescribed or to administer them on the spot when required. Only one single table for pharmacy could fit in the limited space at the rear end of the canopy, barely in the shade. It was well under way of being set up but due to lack of space, not all the supplies could be laid out, instead many of the boxes had to remain on the ground, underneath the table

I began to look for a space where I could work and found that the only suitable spot was on the grass in the sun, between the pharmacy table and the water filter table. There seemed to be a shortage of chairs too, so I took some from the rows that had already been set up near the pink building. Due to a large rock protruding out of the grass, I could only fit three chairs, at a push because I needed to cover that rock with a chair or else it would have been tripping me up all day.

The prayer team was spread around in different areas on the perimeter of the canopy, in the sun and without chairs. Joan, our prayer warrior, found a low wall partly shaded area, which she made use of to sit on while praying. The only problem was that the wall bordered an open cow shed, and on the other side of it was a huge, black cow.

Of course, I was curious to see if the cow might become a bit of a challenge. My curiosity got the better of me and on one occasion when I heard extremely loud and repetitive lowing sounds coming from the cow shed, I rushed to see what was going on. I observed Joan praying with her eyes closed and the cow, just a meter away from her head. The cow was lowing so loudly that it began to drown out Joan's voice but Joan, was totally unfazed. She seemed oblivious to the proximity of the cow and simply continued praying.

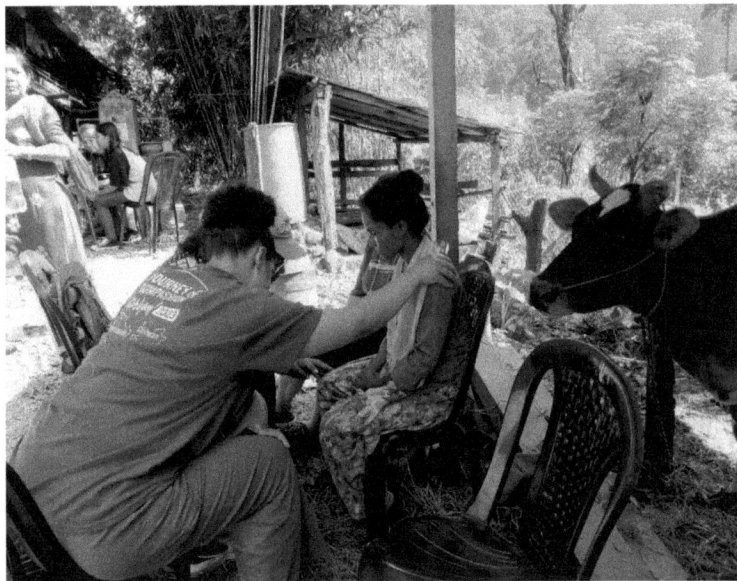

SACRED PRAYER WITH ONLOOKING COW

The louder the cow lowed, the louder she prayed, and each time with more authority. The way she handled it was commendable; she was determined not to be distracted by that noisy cow and remained incredibly focused. Eventually, when the cow gave in and became silent, Joan carried on praying, but in her normal voice and with an ear-to-ear smile that radiated with joy and satisfaction.

The toilet facilities for everyone, including the locals, stood at the very back of the site. It consisted of a singular free-standing shed with the strangest looking porcelain toilet bowl cemented into a concrete slab on the ground. Inside the tiny dunny was a bucket of water and a plastic bag, but no toilet roll. I had brought my own toilet paper and I was grateful that I didn't have to go in the bush, but still, it took some getting used to.

I stood in the pharmacy area and looked at the activity all around me. I could clearly see an extremely busy clinic, chairs filled with people and even more standing in line waiting to be attended to. I perceived that God was already at work in this little green space under heaven and I began to believe for nothing less than miracles of healing and restoration that day.

Basanta arrived and greeted me with enthusiasm, we had come to know each other well and I was happy to be able to work with him on our last clinic day. I explained that my role had changed and instead of diagnosing and treating, I was to explain the medicines and doses that had been prescribed.

We instantly dropped into easy dialogue, but our conversation quickly came to an end at the arrival of our first patient. Shirisha, a young woman in her early twenties, had a Ventolin nebuliser in her hand; she had been diagnosed with chronic asthma by one of the clinic doctors. Shirisha had never come across this type of medication before and wasn't sure how to use it. I carefully described the method of use and it seemed like Basanta was explaining everything very clearly. However, when I asked Shirisha to self-administer one puff of Ventolin to show me that she had understood what to do, she shook her head and shyly refused. I felt that she had not grasped the technique, so I explained to Basanta that I needed her to demonstrate her understanding by taking a puff herself. After many words from Basanta, Shirisha remained silent in a painfully shy moment. Her cheeks blushed bright red revealing her embarrassment and there were people all around us. I waited, then in a quiet way, Shirisha finally asked, almost in a whisper, if we could explain again how to use it.

After more explicit instruction, this time with much more graphic demonstrations of activating the spray into the air to show how to release the medication, and with exaggerated inhalations demonstrated by both myself as well as Basanta, Shirisha was willing to give it a go. She gave herself a puff of Ventolin and managed it very well. After some encouragement she administered a second puff with more confidence. She had finally got it and Shirisha walked off with a triumphant smile on her face. It seemed like a great win for all of us.

We had taken so long attending to Shirisha that the area was becoming congested with no room for a queue to form. Many people were randomly standing in wait and were crowding in on the only three chairs occupied by Basanta, myself and the person we were attending. Without a queue it was difficult to know who was next. But the gracious Nepali people were so respectful that they simply gave way to one another and insisted that the other go first. There were never any disputes as they were also able to accept the gracious offer of the one giving in.

SERVING CURRY & RICE

Fortunately, the medications to be administered were mainly analgesics, antibiotics or multivitamins which were much more straightforward and easier to explain. Eventually the congestion became more manageable as we ploughed through the crowd. Then suddenly, once the lunch announcement was made, all that were still waiting, quickly hurried off to get fed. Basanta and I just looked at each other in surprise and decided that we may as well join them.

Hardly anyone had asked for prayer in the pharmacy,

probably due to the numerous amounts of people still waiting to be seen. I was glad to hear however that a good number had been directed to the prayer team from the clinic staff.

Later that evening in the debriefing session, we heard many testimonies from various team members who had actually witnessed a woman's blind eyes being opened. Another testimony was that of a man in the village who was the Shaman (the Witch Doctor) of the village. After being healed, this man had come to a saving faith in Christ as did a number of others, who had grasped the Gospel message for the first-time and had made a commitment to follow Jesus.

Chapter Sixteen

EYEWITNESS ACCOUNTS

TESTIMONY – JOAN GREENFIELD - *Healing in a Remote Mountain Village*

he day started out early as it always does with breakfast, then prayer and worship. How critical the prayer and worship are to everything we do! I was still feeling a little unwell but was determined to go and minister in our last clinic. After a long bus ride, some walking up the mountain and a welcome ride for some of us in the truck bringing the medical bags, we arrived at our destination, a remote mountain village named Rapti. There was a small group of people gathering as we prepared for the clinic. They welcomed and honored us with beautiful leis that they had made with the local flowers and leaves. How special!

Once the clinic started the prayer teams began to pray for people and healing broke out among these precious people! Many were healed of pain and touched by the love of God. I will share three testimonies that most touched me from this day.

There was an elderly woman who was brought to our prayer station walking with a large stick and accompanied by a couple of her young grandchildren. We were told that she was blind and she indicated that she could only see black. As our team prayed, she started to get some near vision and could distinguish how many fingers we were holding up, but when we moved further away, she indicated that everything was blurry. We did not feel that God was finished with healing her, but other people were waiting for prayer so I took her over to Pastor Adam and asked him if he could continue praying for her. By the time he and others were finished she had her vision back and even needed sunglasses as the light was too bright!

Another older man was brought to us who we were told had an alcohol problem and liver issues. We prayed for his health and that he would be able to stop drinking. Then he told us that he used to go to the little church where we were doing the clinic and asked us about a dream that he had been having repeatedly where the pastor came to him in the dream holding a little milk and a little soil and offering it to him. He wondered what it meant.

Immediately I thought of the words in Isaiah.

'Is anyone thirsty? Come and drink, even if you have no money! Come, take your choice of wine or milk, it's all free! Why spend your money on food that does not give you strength? Why pay for food that does you no good? Listen to me, and you will eat what is good. You will enjoy

*the finest food, Come to me with your ears wide open.
Listen, and you will find life.'*

(Isaiah 55:1-3)

I told him that Jesus was drawing him back to faith and was asking him to choose light instead of darkness and life instead of death. To choose Jesus! He indicated that he wanted to follow Jesus and prayed a prayer of recommitment. He said he planned to go back to the little church and we took down his name for the local pastor to connect with him.

The third testimony from that clinic that I would like to share is that of a man who wanted prayer for his arm. From what the translator shared after talking to him, I believe that he had pain and limited use in his arm due to a work-related injury. After we prayed for him, the pain was gone and he was moving his arm back and forth like he was cutting rice with a scythe. With joy he indicated that it was healed!

I felt to tell him that Jesus had healed him and asked if he would like to know more about Jesus, and he indicated that he would. I introduced him to one of our local doctors who shared the good news of the gospel with him and the man told the doctor that he had been thinking of becoming a Christian for a long time and when he was healed the time was right!

These are just three of the wonderful things that happened on that glorious day! What a privilege to be a part of it!

Joan Greenfield

JOAN GREENFIELD

<u>*TESTIMONY – RANDEEP MATTHEWS*</u> - *A Journey of Compassion*

Our journey into the heart of the mountains began with a shared sense of purpose and a commitment to make a difference. Accompanied by our friends from different nations, team of local translators, Doctors, Nurses and Pastoral team, we set out to reach a remote village that had been largely untouched by the outside world. The roads were treacherous, winding through steep mountains and dense forests, but our determination fuelled us as we navigated each dangerous turn.

As we drove deeper into the mountains, the scenery transformed into breathtaking vistas, but the path ahead was riddled with challenges. The roads were narrow and rugged, and at times, we had to manoeuvre around landslides and obstacles that nature had thrown our way. Yet, with every bump and jolt, our resolve only grew stronger.

Upon arriving in the village, we were greeted by warm smiles and open hearts, despite the hardships the community faced. To my surprise, these very simple people, with very little to offer, hosted us with genuine hospitality. They welcomed us into their village and shared with us their life, embodying a spirit of generosity that left a lasting impression on us.

We listened intently, learning about their daily lives, the lack of resources, and the challenges they encountered in accessing basic necessities. Fuelled by compassion, we set to work. We set up our medical camp and people were given medicines according to their needs. We distributed food, water filters, and essential supplies, but it was the connections we made that truly mattered. We shared laughter, stories, and hope, forging bonds that transcended language and culture.

One poignant moment stood out during our time there. A local witch doctor, who had come to observe our activities, experienced a sudden pain in his stomach. In that moment of vulnerability, he was confronted with the power of God. We prayed for him, inviting the healing presence of Jesus into his life. To our amazement, he was completely healed, and in that transformative moment, he gave his life to the Lord.

This experience reaffirmed the belief of many in the team, belief that God has a great plan for that village. I am

confident that the small church there will be used power-
fully to bring salvation and hope to the entire community.
As we prepared to leave, the villagers expressed their grati-
tude, but it was us who felt truly blessed.

Our journey into that remote village taught us invalu-
able lessons about resilience, kindness, and the power of
community. It reminded us that compassion knows no
boundaries and that sometimes, the most challenging paths
lead to the most rewarding experiences. This journey was
not just a mission; it was a testament to the unwavering
spirit of humanity, showing us that, together, we can
weather any storm and uplift one another in times of need.

Randeep Mathews

TESTIMONY – GREG BONNER – One Man

Anyone who grew up in 1960s Australia will understand
that talking about stuff like feelings or emotions still feels
strange, even in the postmodernist, self-absorbed 2020s.
Here goes anyway!

One day in mid-2023, I returned home from whatever,
to be greeted by an effervescent Bridget.

'Guess what?' she blurted out excitedly.

I've learned over the years that the 'guess what' ques-
tion often means something significant so I listened.
Bridget mentioned a friend of hers, Lesley, who had shared
about her recent 'Journey of Compassion,' trip. This really
hit a chord with her and invoked some serious interest.

When I asked her to explain what a JOC was, she
handed me a book and said, 'Will you read this; the

founder wrote it and it's interesting.' A few days later, before I was even halfway into the book, Bridget presented with another enthusiastic, 'Guess where the next JOC is going.'

'Tell me… where?' I responded.

'Nepal!' she said, waiting eagerly for my response.

I took a minute to think, not being sure if I was excited or challenged. True I'd been to Nepal five times before; I loved the culture and the ways of the people but Prayer and Healing? Really … me? Sure, I like prayer in small numbers, like one or two but the thought of praying openly surrounded by people and maybe using prayer to heal someone, well I'd feel more comfortable abseiling or swimming with sharks.

I didn't want to think too deeply about this so I answered, "Well let's just do it!" Maybe I can stay with the 'Water Filter Team,' or take on 'Crowd Control.'

We found ourselves in Kathmandu, not before too long. Of course, there had been many things to do before leaving the Central Coast but looking back, time passed quickly. We joined the multinational team of Canadians, Brits, Yanks and Aussies, all good!

We had a Praise and Worship Session that day and (perhaps surprisingly) it felt so natural. To be sure everyone will worship in their own way and I've learnt not to have many expectations: Australian Baptists tend to be very quietly expressive while Australian Pentecostals can appear to be really "out there". This new group seemed steadily grounded, definitely involved and joyous. Moreover, there was a sense of togetherness, as if we were all born of the same heart and mind. It felt wholesome and wonderful.

The next 48 hours became a mixture of training mixed with a little sightseeing. Cultural awareness, and realistic expectations were emphasised. On the second day, we were advised which groups we would be working in. Imagine the dread I felt, when told I would be on the Prayer Team: I mean – 'Seriously? Me? Surely, somebody else ...'. In short, I felt thoroughly 'under-gunned'. I actually considered speaking with Bill Verbakel and explaining that I would be far more useful assembling water filters; but I didn't.

I slept fitfully, in part because the hotel fronted onto a very busy and noisy intersection which attracted people with late night business to do, political activists and itinerant workers and in part because I struggled with my upcoming duty. I felt somewhat numb going to breakfast and exchanging greetings with the others. I didn't linger but went back to my room and prayed.

My prayer, although sincere, didn't seem to change my state, so then I opened my bible app. I recalled something that came up during one of our worship meetings ... something about Jesus having compassion on the people. When I read Mark 6:34, I stopped. It was like time stopped. I felt like I was looking at the people gathering by the sea, aimless, hot and bothered, sheep without a shepherd ... and I felt compassion, deep compassion.

This changed everything for me: I wasn't in Southern Nepal to perform wonders; I didn't need to prove anything at all. It wasn't about me; It was about them.

Later that day we went to a village in a long green valley. There was a church or assembly hall and there were people, some in Western work clothes, others in traditional clothing. The older ones seemed bent over from a lifetime

*of heavy loads, the younger women overburdened by chil-
dren, the younger men weighed down by long hard days in
the field or injuries or something spiritual…a mixture of
believers and non-believers … all needing something … that
feeling of compassion struck me again, only harder.*

*Initially, I was teamed up with older and wiser prayers
and they would ask what the person wanted. They would
carefully and patiently listen to the sufferer's story (per an
interpreter) and then offer prayer and ask permission to
touch the injured part or lay a hand on their shoulder. After
the prayer, questions would be asked and tests applied to
see if there was any real difference. If not, more prayer was
offered, sometimes by the same experienced prayer or
somebody else might be called to pray, and sometimes I
was asked to pray.*

*Later, I would pray by myself but with an interpreter,
usually a Nepalese younger person (and these were excel-
lent in terms of language skills and understanding). To
begin with, of course I was more than curious to see if the
Lord might actually be healing people or whether the
people were just being polite when they were saying, "the
pain is gone." I even considered whether something
psycho-symptomatic might be happening.*

*I remember a middle-aged woman with a terribly sore
and weakened knee. When the interpreter Maya said, "She
is cured." I asked Maya to have her walk, then to crouch,
then squat. She was fine.*

*Later a younger mother wanted prayer for her 9-month-
old, who was listless, semi-conscious and burning up. I
prayed and nothing changed so I asked Maya to pray while
I observed. A minute after she began, it was as if a light
went on in the child. He suddenly looked at me directly in*

the eyes, then he turned his head to look at Maya, then his mother. He was immediately alert and cried strongly.

By that stage I was no longer focussed on results ... I stopped trying to keep score and instead I focussed on caring for the people. There seemed to be an unending stream of people but it hardly mattered, I was now doing what I was supposed to do, what we are all supposed to (and can) do, being prepared to be that conduit between the one suffering and the one who will provide an easing or a curing.

I will go again.

Gregory Bonner

TESTIMONY - BASANTA PAHARI - Translator

My name is Basanta Pahari. I am seventeen years old and I live in Kathmandu, Nepal. I was a translator with the Impact Nations team in Chitwan, Nepal. This was one of the best memorable moments of my life. I was stunned because I belong to a Hindu family and I didn't know much about Jesus. But with the team, I got to know so much about Jesus and I saw miracles of people recovering with the power of praying to Jesus, which changed so many lives including mine. Our eyes were opened.

I was absolutely stunned. Since then, I pray to Jesus every day. The amazing work that the Impact Nations team did, and the way they treated us, with love and respect, makes me feel so good. I got to learn so many things from Bridget, like knowledge about medications and also about Jesus.

I wish and pray for Bridget and the team to succeed in every project and I pray that God fulfill all your needs and provide a happy, healthy and successful life. In the name of Jesus, Amen.

Basanta Pahari

TESTIMONY – DEB RUNSTEDLER - For this a very special journey!

I arrived a few days before the Journey of Compassion with Impact Nations commenced and I was able to travel to the Northern region of Nepal to meet with my foster child and her family. As a result, the most impactful thing that happened for me, was when a sponsored girl from the 'Center,' gave her testimony. The young girl said that before she was sponsored, she had no hope for the future but that now she has hope. Instantly I recalled my foster child from the recent visit and this comment touched me deeply. The Bible reveals that God says: 'My people perish without hope.'

I believe that this journey was all about bringing hope to the people of Nepal and showing them that God sees them and that He loves them.

Deb Runstedler

DEB & JOAN PRAYING

TESTIMONY – SUE BRAUND

Nepal JOC-our first JOC adventure after hearing about and interceding for so many others.

What was the real purpose for me to be there? Was it to be the hands and feet of Christ serving the small villages we visited - or was there a different and more personal reason for me to be there?

A year later, the most outstanding memory was that Scriptures came alive – almost appearing in three dimensions from a previous two-dimensional shadow. It spoke into my spirit in such a magnificent way. It framed the breath of God we were experiencing. It spoke vision.

'And I myself will be a wall of fire around it,' declares the Lord, 'And I will be its glory within.'
> *Zechariah 2:5 (English Standard Version ESV)*

We had a dear friend at home fighting a deadly stage 4 cancer. So wretched did he feel, that he said his goodbyes to my husband as we left - he wasn't sure he'd survive the chemo! As we travelled to Nepal he was deeply in our thoughts and prayers - to the point that he literally became my prayer focus. Such were the Scripture references that flooded our days listening to teaching and being challenged to focus on Kingdom things. Ps 116 would leap into being and the promises seemed to be for our friend. Texts became solid and full of purpose.

On one occasion, as I texted the truth about the Gospel promises to our friend, I felt it lacked authority – this was no time for well-meaning platitudes! I asked our team leader to help me pray. He texted our friend:

> *'You carry everlasting life in you so command your body to come into alignment to the everlasting life in you. Remember the one who is in you is greater than the one who is in the world.'*

The truth of this resonated so strongly – I needed to get into alignment with the eternal life I hold in Christ.

> *Consecrate yourselves for tomorrow the Lord will do wonders among you.*
>> *Joshua 3:5 (ESV)*

These words were unbelievably uplifting. In the words of Jesus 'Follow me' or reiterated, come into alignment with me. This was less about obedience than coming into a realisation of who we are and what Kingdom purposes of Christ were there for us to be focused on. And we go on a JOC to pray faith for a brother back home! God is amazing!

Our friend shot a text back to us,

'Hi Sue, yesterday I was admitted with very high temp and pulse, red cells badly diminished & white cells almost gone (10 down to 0.3) my ability to fight infection was so compromised I was in danger of sepsis which I'm told is very hard to come back from. I did keep breathing through a long night and prayed to our father to save my life. I'm still here today in hospital and with the help of wonderful doctors my bloods are heading in the right direction though not out of the woods. I asked God to just give me something to hang on to and as I dozed, I dreamt of a picture in a children's bible that mum gave as a seven-year-old in 1969. I hadn't seen it for a long time but it was imprinted in a corner of my mind. I started to believe I'll beat this. Such a strange path I'm on; to be facing death to understand how to live. Thank you so much for every text and prayer, they lift me up and give me hope.'

What a blessing! We had to go to Nepal to receive this sort of Spirit updraft. He is still fighting the disease but now with solid faith that Jesus is surrounding and holding him.

But the truth of the gospels became a reality in a sad way too. JOC's are full of opportunities to pray for people to be healed and some are not. So, we continue to be challenged to come into alignment with the kingdom and persevere in prayer. A gift from the Nepal JOC that lives on. It was on this Journey of Compassion that opportunities both unique and glorious emerged and spoke into my spirit. Such was my experience.

Sue Braund

Chapter Seventeen

FAREWELL NEPAL

23rd October 2023

*I*n the subtropical climate of Chitwan, the beautiful Nepalese people, in their small remote villages at the foot of the Himalayas, experienced a touch from heaven. How could they explain the healings that took place or the changed hearts, I wondered? But in my own heart, I know the answer. Only God! I prayed, God answered, and I saw people healed in powerful ways. I believe that God used every one of us, but it was God alone that brought about the healings. He brought relief as a result of the medical clinics and even the water filters, but we had the privilege of experiencing a closer relationship with Him as well as the humility of the people and their respectful culture. I really loved this Journey of Compassion! I hope and pray that I can go again and again.

The time to leave Chitwan was fast approaching. It was only at the Farewell Dinner on our final night, during the concluding speeches, when it hit me that our Journey of Compassion had come to a close! I could hardly believe it was over, our ten days had slipped away so very quickly, and I began to feel melancholic, not wanting this JOC to end.

We all pitched in to provide a small gift which was presented to each of the translators. They shed a tear or two, by their emotional response we could see that they were touched and were obviously feeling as sentimental as the rest of us.

After much reflection that night (see epilogue), I drifted into a very peaceful sleep having a wonderfully restful night's sleep. Unfortunately, not so for Greg, our last celebratory meal did not agree with him and he suffered terribly from gastro during the night. The next morning Greg was so tired, nevertheless he soldiered on throughout our time of worship and the debriefing session.

After the Nepali component of the team paid their final farewells, we set off. The long bus ride back to Kathmandu was filled with silence. Most of the journey was spent with each contemplating their own thoughts. It was only the noise and the chaos of that familiar city which alerted us of our arrival in Thamel. The best part of the day was gone and we spent our last sleepless night at the Northfield Hotel.

From then on, we each went our own way. Some needed to return home very early the next day for work commitments, others (retirees) had the luxury of spending more leisure time post JOC. Elizabeth was staying longer in Kathmandu to volunteer with an altogether different organisation. Out of our Aussie group, only Beck was due back for work and family commitments, however Anne and Arthur (although senior citizens), had decided to return home with Beck. The rest of the retirees, Lesley & Barry, Sue & Murray and myself and Greg, had decided to spend some down-time in the tourism capital of Nepal, Pokhara. We managed to book the same flight on Jeti Airlines which took less than half an hour on a very small aircraft. The flight was by no means smooth. Peering out the window we were spellbound by the natural beauty of the landscape with its spectacular backdrop of awe-inspiring Annapurna Mountains. They seemed to get bigger and bigger until, with a tremendous thump, the spell was broken as the craft made it's touch down.

We recovered from the shock of landing almost as soon as we set foot on the tarmac. The ambience of the airport was starkly different to that of Kathmandu. A calm relaxed vibe permeated the pristine air and the temperature felt a few degrees warmer with a pleasantly cool breeze. Perhaps that's why Pokhara is known as 'the Jewel of the Himalayas'.

Once settled in and fed at the Hotel Jal Mahal, on the outskirts of Pokhara, Greg and I spent our first evening walking around the streets and interacting with the very friendly locals. Pokhara is known for its low crime rate and the whole country was in the middle of celebrating the biggest and most widely celebrated Hindu festival of Dashain. Dashain is a time of joy and merriment and symbolises the victory of good over evil, we felt pretty safe. The warmth of the local people resonated as they approached and initiated conversation with us; some just wanted to practice their English, others with very little English still attempted to communicate with us.

I will never forget the interaction we had with a bunch of ladies wearing elaborate red saris. As we were passing by, they stopped us in our tracks and in very broken English, all at once, they said, 'Happy Dashain,' and then burst into giggles like embarrassed teenagers. Irresistibly, we were drawn in by their contagious laughter and a conversation began.

They seemed curious, but they spoke in Nepalese and we had no idea what they were saying to us, then one young woman asked, 'Where from you?' with a strong Nepali accent. We both responded, 'Australia.'

Another uproar of laughter erupted, amidst which, an older lady excitedly raised her voice above the others exclaiming indecipherable words. They were quickly translated, 'My son lives in Sydney.' After much nodding of heads in affirmation, each woman introduced herself and one of them introduced the little boy she was carrying. He was so cute, barely one year old, yet dressed in a traditional outfit including a Topi.

The conversation continued with much hilarity. The ladies sang to us and they even danced for us, Bollywood style, and when they did, the little boy joined in with all the arm and hand moves. We were encouraged to join in. I made an attempt but Greg drew the line; Bollywood dancing was a definite 'no go zone' for him.

The next day we joined the others in central Pokhara and checked into the Middle Path Hotel where they were staying for another two nights. During that time, we did some short walks and visited a few of Pokhara's sightseeing spots including Seti River Gorge, Jangchub Choeling Tibetan Monastery, and the Annapurna Cable Car. Our time together was well spent relaxing and reflecting on the previous ten days. As you might expect the moment to part company with our Aussie friends had fast approached and we said our farewells.

DINNER WITH FRIENDS IN POKHARA

Our attention quickly turned to the trek we had planned to Poon Hill and we became very excited about it. It was a five-day trekking experience covering 62km in altitude ranging from 800m to 3,210m. That night I was drawn by the rich inviting aroma of curry and we dined in a typical Nepali restaurant. Greg had just overcome his upset stomach and stayed clear of the curries, whereas I enjoyed a very tasty one. However, its effect was like the venom of a snake and it did not end well. I spent a very unpleasant night as it made a dynamic exit from both ends of my gastrointestinal tract!

After a horrific and sleepless night, the long-awaited trek was about to begin but the excitement was all but gone for me. I felt only fear and trepidation, wondering how on earth I was going to do it. The major concern in my mind was, 'Am I going to make it from one 'squat latrine' to another?'

Tara, our friend and faithful guide from way back, suggested that I should go back to bed and rest for a few hours before setting off. He explained that it was a steep uphill climb on rugged Himalayan paths to our first stop in Ghorepani. Tara suggested that we could take a jeep and drive for an hour or so to make up for lost time. I was sold … all I wanted to do was to lay down and be as still as a corpse on my bed.

The jeep took us uphill over a narrow gravel road for some distance, larger loose stones constantly hit off the mud guards. We passed Nepalese people with small bodies carrying heavy, bulky loads on their backs in straw baskets, supported only by a band around their head. Chickens would occasionally run ahead of the jeep, frantically flapping their wings to escape being splattered, but with nowhere to run. They did somehow manage to make it back to the safety of their abode, often a brightly coloured tea house not too far ahead. The jolting around was only made tolerable by the medication I had taken and I was so relieved to step back onto firm ground.

The path consisted mainly of steps which seemed to go on and on in a relentlessly upward gradient. The steps were made up of large stone slabs which had been laid side by side. On the very steep sections it got really tough and after an hour of continuously negotiating the gruelling, irregular uphill steps, I was lagging behind by a longshot.

I felt hot, tired and about to bust, not sure if I could make it to the next latrine. I looked up and, in the distance, I saw the men waiting at the top of the steps. I could also see a Tea House off to the side, close behind them; this was the exact incentive I needed to make me hang on and pick up my pace. Just at the critical time, I reached the Tea House and made a beeline for the latrine, only to find that the single public latrine was occupied.

Tara grabbed the owner's arm as he walked by, I don't know what he said, but I found myself being rushed inside the home to the personal toilet of the owner. Instantly, in the nick of time, my bowels erupted. What a dreadful feeling, but at the same time, what a relief!

Even after a cool drink of water and a short rest, there was no way I could continue. Tara had to rethink our strategy. We ended up spending the night at the Tea House and the next morning, with the help of more medication and a reasonable night's sleep, I was feeling better. We set off all feeling reenergised, but after the first five-hundred or so steps, with a banging headache and very shaky legs, I was ready to keel over.

Tara had to reevaluate the situation once again, and He gave me two options... either turn back or continue forward on horseback! By then, I was finding it difficult to breath but it was even more difficult for me to give in. Horseback it had to be; horseback it was! Tara and Greg continued on ahead while I sat on a rock and waited for our sherpa to return with a horse. It seemed like a long time in the solitude of my own company. Only the sound of birds chirping, rushing water and the occasional buzz of a solitary mosquito became larger-than-life sounds that broke the silence.

I spent the time talking to God. Then I asked Him to bring healing to my body and to help me not to feel too humiliated when the horse arrived. I also glanced at my phone to glean some encouragement from the prayers sent by the prayer-cover group on the WhatsApp. Knowing that people were praying for us was so good at that particular moment. The thought, 'Many are the plans of man,' echoed in my mind at that point, and I asked God to show me what it was He wanted me to learn from this experience.

TIKA THE HORSE

On mounting the horse called 'Tika', it wasn't humiliating at all, instead, I was feeling very grateful and at the same time very humbled. It crossed my mind that, perhaps those were the two qualities that God wanted to grow in me.

POON HILL VIEWING PLATFORM

On arrival at Ghoripani, around 3pm, the temperature had dropped to six degrees. I was at the point of exhaustion and went straight to bed. It was so cold I slept in my clothes, plus a thermal jacket and I was still shivering under the heavy doona. Eventually I warmed up and slept soundly until the next day around 2pm. Even though I was feeling much better, Tara insisted that we stay a second night in Ghoripani before tackling the final section of the trek.

Tara knew that the forty minute trek ahead of us would take a lot longer for me, so to catch the sun rising, we set off in the dark at 4am the next morning. Another five hundred steps further up and we finally reached the platform of Poon Hill at an altitude of 3,200m. The vista over Nepal's Annapurna snowcapped mountain range was absolutely stunning! To see that first glimpse of brilliant light appearing beyond the dark silhouette of the mountains, gradually increase in size, was awe inspiring. A magnificent golden glow slowly illuminated the entire mountain range in such glorious splendour, it was breathtaking! The impressive sunrise rewarded all our efforts and from the viewing tower, we could see as far as Mustang. It was definitely well worth it!

Apart from the pleasure of descending 3,767 stone steps, we enjoyed walking on trails through rhododendron forests and passing many waterfalls surrounded by beautiful panoramic scenery. The delightful tea houses in Tadapani and Chomrong and the natural hot springs in Jhinu Danda with bubbling therapeutic mineral water were all very relaxing experiences along the way.

On return to Pokhara with another four nights to go, we checked into the Majestic Lake Front Hotel. Our days were filled with new and exciting experiences. The Nepalese Momo, a delightful bite-sized dumpling, is one of our favourite comfort foods so we booked into a workshop to learn how to make them. Nepalese Momos are traditionally made with a thin, doughy wrapper filled with a savory mixture of chicken mince with added spices and onion. Greg and I rediscovered just how opposite our personalities are. I made every effort to produce perfectly shaped and uniformly sized Momo's, while Greg, no matter how much instruction he received from the chef, or what I tried to show him, produced a mishmash of unrecognisable lumps of dough on the tray ... it was most frustrating, his Momo's nearly gave me grounds for divorce … but it was a lot of fun too. The chef described Greg's Momos as 'overworked stress balls!'

The highlight of our experiences was when we decided, on the day before our return flight, to partake in a Bungie Jump over the Kali Gandaki River. The beautiful Himalayan landscape was backdrop to a deep gorge with furious waters rushing around huge boulders randomly scattered along its course below. Greg jumped first and not only conquered his fear of heights, but he made it look easy as he dived headfirst into a graceful free fall all the way down. I stepped towards the edge of the platform and looking 100 meters below, my heart pounded with excitement. The adrenalin was pumping as I took a run and jump … wow!! It certainly was the most exhilarating thrill I've ever had.

I enjoyed every moment of our Journey of Compassion. Both the journey and the jump were a tremendous leap of faith … perhaps God willing, we will get the opportunity to experience another JOC and another leap of faith in a different corner of the globe.

EPILOGUE

My first Journey of Compassion turned out to be much more than I had expected. On reflection, I realise that it had not only had a profoundly personal impact on myself, but it had an impact on each member of the team and on the community we served. That tiny remote church had been deeply influenced by the healings which took place and by the new citizens added to the Kingdom. The shared cross-cultural awareness and understanding of love, compassion, forgiveness and mercy, were profound. This priceless, shared understanding made the whole experience worthwhile.

I struggled with 'laying down my rights' during the landslide, and I grappled with unanswered prayer, both encounters resulted in personal growth. I experienced meeting and working with like-minded people from across the globe and the challenge in the early morning teaching sessions with Randeep at the start of every day. I Shared thoughts with Elizabeth on the prayer walks and with other team members over breakfast. I will forever remember the times when heaven seemed to come down and touch Earth during our worship sessions. Seeing with my own eyes that people were healed and feeling the disappointment that others were not. Experiencing the joy of lives changed for all eternity … all of it had left an incredible impression on me, and somehow, it was all so wholesomely stretching and enriching. The recollection of these experiences will perpetuate in my memory forever. I will keep on partaking in further Journeys of Compassion for as long as the power of the Holy Spirit enables me.

Investing into God's kingdom is a good thing, but I've discovered…it's more than just putting your hand into your pocket, that's far too easy, it's nowhere near as rewarding and the returns are negligible. However, being God's hands and feet on the ground, is much more satisfying, and the returns are enormous despite the challenge and the cost. Nothing really compares to being an eyewitness experiencing the work of the Holy Spirit firsthand.

This journey has taken me beyond the range of merely physical human experience. Yes…each day challenged me with a whole bunch of things to do, but it wasn't just the 'doing', it was the 'being.' Abiding in Christ, co-working with Him, being fully dependent on the Holy Spirit to enable me to walk in step with God. I was energised at the end of each mission day, instead of feeling exhausted, I walked away, three inches off the ground looking forward to the next day. Surely there must be a connection with 'being' and 'doing' that results in action, both physical and spiritual. It's a mystery that I can't quite fathom and I've ceased trying to understand but I am left wanting to follow the wisdom of the scriptures and to offer my hands and feet to further the Kingdom of God.

Trust in the Lord with all your heart; do not depend on your own understanding.

(Proverbs 3:5)

I believe with all my heart that God has written a different narrative for me than he has for you. You might be called to impact 'your' home community. Steve Stewart might be called to reach the nations. I believe I am called to be God's hands and feet wherever in the world I find myself. Self-sacrifice is the way God shows us our true selves (Matt 16:26 and Luke 9:24). Let's embrace God's calling, and live a life aligned with Christ's example.

For a long, long time, in fact the past thirty-seven years, it has been enough for me to believe without seeing. My beliefs have sustained me, but now I long to see more and to experience more of the work of the Holy Spirit not from a distance, but up close and personal.

Finding the purpose for which God has called us to, and walking in it, is in my opinion, the greatest adventure of a lifetime!

Then Jesus went to work on his disciples. "Anyone who intends to come with me has to let me lead. You're not in the driver's seat; I am. Don't run from suffering; embrace it. Follow me and I'll show you how. Self-help is no help at all. Self-sacrifice is the way, my way, to finding your-self, your true self. What kind of deal is it to get every-thing you want but lose yourself? What could you ever trade your soul for?

(Matthew 16:26 The Message Bible MSG)

FINAL THOUGHTS: GREG BONNER

A Kinesiologist once told me that walking, because it involves diagonal movement, is great for thinking. After our work in Chitwan we went trekking in the Annapurna's, so this allowed plenty of time to make sense of this latest volunteer work.

I had arrived in Nepal hoping to keep my equilibrium and not getting swayed too much by group emotions or getting over involved in prayer (especially prayers of healing). I just expected and wanted to help, especially with basic stuff like assembling water filters. Instead, I found myself very moved by the deep feeling of connectedness in mutual prayer and worship with total strangers. Instead, I found myself entering the homes of local Nepalese and being asked to pray for sick or seriously injured people even carefully touching their damaged bodies. How was it that some people actually appeared to be healed? How do I make sense of this?

Of course, the Bible instructs us not to lean on our own understanding. But to leave it at that, will not satisfy the mind, that is God given. Equally, scientific methodology requires repeatability, observation and peer review; not a good measure for things of the mind or the spirit. University training taught me about logical thinking, critical thinking and statistics; again, not much help. What about philosophy and legal evidence as suggested by C.S. Lewis ... maybe!

After some days, I realised I was going down the wrong track (emotionally and logically). What's the most exciting thing a human can witness? A miracle. Whether it's a thing of healing or redemption or survival, if it's something that we cannot logically expect or understand, we want to attribute it to our God. I wanted to validate, in my own mind, what I had seen (I guess so I could tell others – I had seen a miracle - so exciting).

I suppose that's OK, so long as I don't mislead myself or others. But what good is it if misleading others is the focus? It is in the end meaningless. Rather, we are instructed to care for the poor, the sick, the foreigner as if for ourselves. The Glory doesn't have anything to do with us, it belongs to God.

A subtle wave of contentment settled on me. I was just doing what every simple person who calls themselves a 'Christian' can do. That was all that mattered, being, for a time, the loving arms of Jesus.

Afterwards, when people would ask me about the experience, I would simply respond by saying that, 'For me I saw things and felt things that I could not easily explain, but that fitted into my understanding of God.' But really, I would continue, 'You need to see for yourself…you need to get out there!'

ABOUT THE AUTHOR

Born in Dublin, into a Catholic family, all that Bridget knew about faith was religion and tradition. Through difficult circumstances in her early teens, Bridget was forced to leave school and disillusioned, she also left the Catholic Church. Her teenage years were spent drifting through a diverse number of jobs, until, out of sheer desperation for somewhere to live, Bridget enrolled into a nursing course, which provided accommodation in the Nurse's Home.

As a mature aged student, Bridget completed a Baccalaureate Degree in Nursing and for many years, found satisfaction in her role on a surgical ward. Over the years, Bridget gained experience in pediatric nursing and psychiatric nursing, as well as becoming a midwife, but eventually she became dissatisfied with nursing altogether.

Searching for new purpose, Bridget studied to become a chaplain. Once qualified, she ministered, firstly within the hospital situation and later to the Red-Light District in her local area.

At the 'empty nest' stage of life, Bridget immersed herself in missionary work. Firstly, in Ecuador for a short period and then in Peru with her husband, Greg, for a period of seven years and, more recently in Nepal.

In between mission work, Bridget wrote her first book, 'The Splendour of a Tear,' a heart rendering account of the plight of the street children in Peru. She continues to enjoy writing true compelling accounts of bringing hope and purpose to those less fortunate.

Bridget and Greg enjoy the great outdoors, kayaking, trekking and skiing but what they love most, is spending time with family.

BIBLIOGRAPHY

Gellner, D. (2007). *Resistance and the State: Nepalese Experiences.* Berghahn Books.

Gurung, K. K. Singh R. (1996). *Chitwan National Park.* Retrieved from Wikipedia: https://en.wikipedia.org/wiki/Chitwan_National_Park

(n.d.). *International Centre for Law and Religion Studies.* International Centre for Law and Religion Studies. Retrieved from https://classic. iclrs.org/content/blurb/files/Nepal.pdf

Koirala, T. (2018). Communicating the Gospel in Nepal. *The Asia Missions Association*, 29th March. Retrieved from https://classic.iclrs. org/content/blurb/files/Nepal.pdf)

Nepal), T. K. (March 29th 2018). The Asia Missions Association: Communicating The Gospel In Nepal.

Piper, J. (1993). *Let the Nations Be Glad: The Supremacy Of God In Missions.* Inter-Varsity Press.

Schmidt, K. J. (20 May 2015). *An Atlas and Survey of South Asian History.* Routledge .

Stewart, S. (2015). *When Everything Changes: Healing, Justice and the Kingdom of God.* Ilinois: Fresh Wind Press.

Stewart, S. (2020). *www.impactnations.com/our-mission.* Retrieved from Impact Nations International Ministries.

ACKNOWLEDGMENTS

I am thankful first to you, my husband Greg, for constantly loving me and patiently supporting me and for all the sacrifices you've made so that I can write. It's an honour to be your wife.

Sari was the first to proofread this book, and despite its rudimentary state Sari encouraged me to continue, and contributed her skills to refine the words a little further. Heather and Pam spurred me on as they continued to hone my work. My brilliant daughter, Carmen and her boundless energy and focus, contributed valuable insights and creativity to the writing, bringing it to its final polished form.

Many have taken the time out of their busy schedules to give a piece of their life and heart in the form of a personal testimony of the miracles they witnessed. These include Joan Greenfield and Deb Runstedler (Canada), Randeep Matthews (India), Greg Bonner, Basanta Pahari (Nepal) and Sue Braund (Australia). A heartfelt thank you to all!

Lastly, but always first in my every day, I honour God for His guidance, strength, and unwavering presence in my life.

OTHER BOOKS BY BRIDGET BONNER

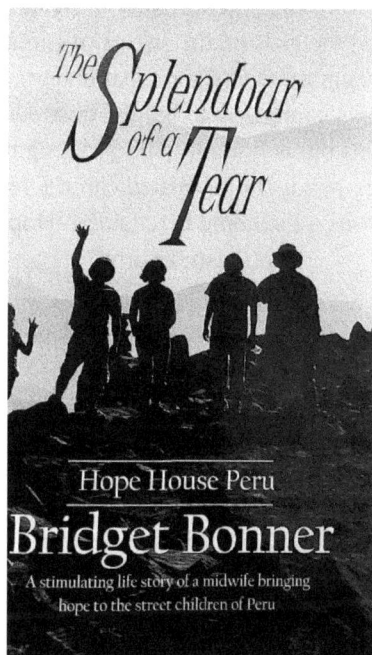

The Splendour of a Tear

Hope House Peru

Bridget Bonner

A stimulating life story of a midwife bringing
hope to the street children of Peru

Everyone has family. This real-life story is about young girls
running away to escape the sad, hostile environment of their
family life. The girls, shaped by the cruelty they refused to accept,
run to the streets hoping to eke out a living as best they can, but
only disappointment is found. Ever optimistic, they keep on
searching for the love they desperately need.

Some chapters include actual journal entries, but the entire
narrative is a true account of what happened as seen through my
eyes. The narrative begins with a child's desperate escape, which
connects with my own subtler story of escape. For all of us, life's
journey involves a kaleidoscope of feelings and emotions almost

impossible to pen. I have endeavoured to paint a picture, using words to carve their way through the landscape of my life, and of theirs.

Surpassing peace, found while meandering through Ecuador, finds a resting place, Peru. Here a gentle flow intricately weaves my life with the lives of the girls on the streets of Lima. Their stories unfold, and I begin to understand what underprivileged really means. I must do something to help! Construction of a place called home begins but is fraught with disappointment and tainted by the shocking betrayal of a trusted carer. Eventually, a new beginning dawns – the home is renamed 'Hope House' and optimism returns.

Coming soon: On the Move: A Journey of Compassion - Africa

ABOUT IMPACT NATIONS

Volunteering overseas can be both rewarding and challenging.
Choosing which organisation to go with can be confusing, and with so
many to choose from, it's easy to feel overwhelmed.
From personal experience, I highly recommend joining a,
'JOURNEY OF COMPASSION'
with
'IMPACT NATIONS,'
Here's why:

- Embark on a Life-Changing Journey with a diverse team
  committed to bringing hope, healing, and practical solutions
  to communities in need.
- Engage in medical clinics, community projects, and
  distribution of water filters that directly benefit vulnerable
  populations.
- Take the opportunity for Personal Growth & Purpose
  through hands-on ministry and moments of deep connection.

**To embark on a journey that
will not only change lives—it will change yours.**
Contact the organisation that has perfected the art of facilitating cross-
cultural missions by guiding volunteers from start to finish.

impactnations
— rescuing lives

www.impactnations.com